ADVANCE PRAISE FOR
POLO LIFE

So you think you want to be 10 goals? Adam Snow and Shelley Onderdonk debunk the "Pretty Woman" image of life as a professional polo player. Their book, *Polo Life: Horses, Sport, 10 and Zen* is an open door into the life of one of America's best polo athletes. Hall-of-Famer Adam Snow and his wife, Shelley Onderdonk, give an overview of Adam's polo career from its beginning to the current day. It offers a detailed look at the life of a travelling professional polo player, including some humble moments, victories, sacrifices and his most important equine partnerships. With unique perspectives from Adam himself, and Shelley in her roles as his wife, the mother of his children, business manager and veterinarian, it is a touching look at the struggles and vulnerabilities, the ups and downs of a dedicated pro. Guided by his sports psychologist, Adam finds navigating his way to eventual retirement may be nearly as difficult as it was working his way to the pinnacle of one of the most difficult sports in the world. Informative footnotes allow any reader, not just polo players, to fully understand and appreciate the couple's efforts over the past 20 years. The book delivers on just what the title promises.

— GWEN RIZZO,
EDITOR & PUBLISHER, *POLO PLAYER'S EDITION*

Not since Abbie Hoffman's *Steal This Book* has a man approached his profession like Adam. With his wife Dr. Shelley Onderdonk and a cast of international characters, this tale takes on a *Roy Rogers and Dale Evans meets Sigmund Freud* all the while exploring the oxymoron "American Polo player."

— SAM MORTON, HORSEMAN AND
AUTHOR OF *WHERE THE RIVERS RUN NORTH*

This book is more than a sports memoir—it's the chronicle of two open-hearted, big-brained people building an unlikely life together by focusing on and cultivating the common ground between them; values, home, mindfulness and respect. It's a love story on a lot of levels; love of one another, of the sport, the horses, home, their children, friends and family. At times, it reads like a new-age spirituality piece, but at others it is downright hilarious and exciting. It is beautifully written—two wonderfully distinct voices find a way to harmonize without denying moments of tension and clash. What I love the most about this book is that there's very little cynicism—you seldom find narrators so prodigiously intelligent and well read who nonetheless choose earnestness. Also, there's something in this book for a wide array of readers—polo and/or horse fans, mindfulness/psych nerds, literature buffs, Modern Love enthusiasts, athletes, scholars and more.

— REBECCA BLOOM, WRITER,
OWNER COMMUNICATIONS BLOOM

Adam and Shelley's *Polo Life* is a breeze of fresh air in the polo scene. Behind the cool-headed polo legend rises a super sensitive soul, and horse and nature lover, who was lucky to find in Shelley a true companion to share a dream and a lifestyle that is not always a walk in the park. The book is inspiring, fun and instructive; it goes from polo to yoga, from quantum physics applied in the search for a great mare to the mental strength necessary for winning games and tournaments. Everything is connected. And at the same time, the book is a poetic journey of the last 30 years of American polo at the highest level, narrated in very simple but powerful prose by its last great hero. A must read for everyone, especially for all the kids who want to become professional polo players.

— JAVIER TANOIRA, 7-GOAL PLAYER, AUTHOR, AND FOUNDER OF ALL PRO POLO LEAGUE, ARGENTINA

Polo Life is an intimate and beautiful portrait of Adam and Shelley's world—it features warm, open and honest narratives by both of them on the successes and challenges of their professional and personal lives.

— ELIZA LEE, PhD, PSYCHOLOGIST

POLO
LIFE

POLO
LIFE

Horses, Sport, 10 and Zen

ADAM SNOW
SHELLEY ONDERDONK, D.V.M.

For information about this title or to order other books
and/or electronic media, contact the publisher:
NHF Press
370 Langdon Rd
Aiken SC 29805
www.pololife.co

ISBNs: 978-0-9975854-2-1 (hardcover)
978-0-9975854-0-7 (softcover)
978-0-9975854-1-4 (eBook)

Printed in the United States of America

Cover and Interior design: 1106 Design

DEDICATION

We would like to dedicate this book to our three sons
Dylan, Nathan, and Aidan
Without whom our journey would be incomplete

CONTENTS

FOREWORD

BY STILIANI CHRONI, PHD

I met Adam Snow in January of 1997 in Wellington, Florida. From the notes of our first meeting, which lasted well over two hours, I wrote the following in a sport psychology article that I recently published in the *Journal Of Excellence*:

> *"During the first hours we spent together, I met a troubled poloist—although he looked darn good on the field and in media presentations—who didn't dare to say out loud that he aspired to become a 10-goal player, who hated his pre-game nervousness, who did not trust himself, his teammates, or the teams he played on, who wanted to control things and teammates, and who was pessimistic when thinking about a polo career. The theme that 'shouted to my face' all the way through our talks was lack of confidence. Most likely, AS's lack of confidence triggered the questioning about himself, his abilities, his horses, and his teammates' skills and abilities. It may also have had a role in the undue fear and nervousness prior to a game, the poor images he would see through his mind's eyes, the*

bad feelings after a game, as well as in his worries of what other people thought of him." (Chroni, 2011, p. 66)

What I did not know back then was that I had just met the most committed and hardworking athlete I would ever work with, even to this day.

It did not take Adam too long to free himself from any reservations and articulate that he wanted to be a 10-goal player, and not just "the best that he could be." When we met, it was only a few months after Adam had been lowered to 7-goals from 8. To me, this meant that he had done some things right, considering that very few players advance to such high handicap ratings. What was key in our work was not to change him—his approach to playing great polo was fairly successful—but only to figure out what was not facilitating his progress at that point in time. I quickly realized that the challenge for him was the absence of structure as we find it in other sports: polo teams do not have coaches; most often teams play together for just one tournament, which may last for only two to three weeks; and the four players may not have regular practices. So for our initial years of work together I focused on assisting Adam in developing a strong belief system in himself, his mounts, and his teams; building this confidence proved to be fundamental for dealing with the pressures, demands, and adversity in polo and in life.

When I met Adam, he was already married and father of one child; as he lived his dream of becoming a 10-goal player, he became father to three sons. This means that in all our years of working together I have seen Adam as a "whole" person, not just as a high-level athlete who needs to score goals and win ride-offs, games and tournaments. Finding balance in his life was imperative, although at times the scale of his life was too heavily tilted towards the polo side. Finding balance in our work—in the timing, content and homework—was also critical. Very often we worked while babysitting or driving one or the other of his sons to school or soccer practices.

What I also did not know back then was that our work would become a career-long collaboration and I would be privileged to support him all the way towards retirement. In my profession, top athletes who reach retirement age are most often left to figure out life after sports with no support; teams and athletes themselves stop paying the sport psychology consultant once the high performance goals are attained and the performance demands withdrawn. This has not been the case with Adam. Once we got past using the forbidden word of "retirement," which took about two years, we continued working the same way we had before. By emphasizing quality in his life, he transitioned from being a full-time, high-goal polo player, to being a part-time, high-goal player, and then to continue loving polo and himself as his handicap dropped. Adam had learned how to find his dream, follow it and do the required work for living it. Just like on the way up the handicap ladder, when "he was claiming each next handicap, he was getting stronger mentally, physically, technically, strategically, and of course horse-wise" (Chroni, 2011, p. 62), he also rode down the ladder strong and composed. Of course he was puzzled at times—most people are not prepared for a new life and career to start in their late forties—but he took the time to unravel this new tangle called life after high-goal polo.

Throughout Adam's life in polo he has been blessed to never be alone. I met Shelley Onderdonk, his wife, only a few weeks after I first met Adam, when she was visiting him in Florida for a long weekend. She was a veterinary student in Athens, Georgia, and the mother of one child at the time. Over the years

Shelley has been Adam's best fan, supporter, friend, caregiver, wife, mother of their children and, of course, his veterinarian.

Shelley has also been the best "devil's advocate" for him and the only one who could put a halt on his obsession with buying new horses. Whenever Adam needed distraction from the pressures of daily life he would go out to look for a new horse. It was a necessity to have great horses (and lots of them!) for playing high-goal polo but it was also his outlet; he would immerse himself in travelling for hours and trying horses in order to give him the quietness he needed for clearing his mind. We did a lot of our work when Adam was out and about on a horse trip—on one of these jaunts I was fortunate to enjoy the majestic lavender fields of England in early summer!

Another thing I couldn't have imagined when I first met Adam in 1997, was how much I would learn from Shelley. I learned from her about motherhood, as she already had two children before I gave birth to my son. But the most precious gift Shelley gave me, without her knowing, was watching her do acupuncture on Adam's horses and observing how peacefully she would stroke a horse's body to detect any tension; it was then that I realized what I wanted for myself—to touch people's lives, the athletes that I would work with, in such a peaceful and sound manner. For me, this has been a present in life.

Shelley's presence in this book brings out exactly who she is: a clear-minded, serene, strong, determined, and brilliantly composed woman. It is a first that an athlete who reached the pinnacle of his sport writes his memoirs together with his wife. Shelley's aspect is the one we never hear about or see in the media, except for snapshots of a happy wife after her husband won a game or competition. But there is so much more hidden behind a wife's smile to the camera after a day's hard work and Shelley did her work, by herself and with Adam. Their "combination" has been a success on and off the field.

In this book, Adam and Shelley share intimate stories that reveal the real picture of how things evolved—with many ups and downs, with great highs and profound low points, as life in general (and in any high-level sport) is not like driving along a highway but rather through mountainous winding roads. One's best bet in a life like this is to fall in love with the high winding roads, not the top of the mountain. Adam and Shelley were in love with horses and with each other. It proved to be their recipe for success.

I hope you will enjoy this ride in the wonderland of high goal polo as much as I did. . . .

—Stiliani "Ani" Chroni, PhD., CC-AASP

CHAPTER I

FORTY GOLDEN HALTERS

"Hello?"

"Mr. Snow?" crackles from long distance over my cell phone.

It is a Saturday in 2009 and I am watching my ten-year-old son play soccer in Congaree, South Carolina. An overseas number usually means the call is polo-related.

"Mr. Snow Adam, the polo player?" The accent is alluring—exotic—but I can't place it. English is certainly the man's second or third language and I hear the properness of a British public school education. *How did this person get my cell number?*

"Yes, it's me."

"Sir, I am Prince Jefri Bahar Bolkiah. I believe we are acquainted."

The first time I had met Prince Jefri, younger brother of the Sultan of Brunei, was in 1990 when I travelled to Brunei to play in a Citibank-sponsored polo event. Dense humidity and a turbaned chauffeur, Haji Hamzaa, met our American team at the airport. The following afternoon before the first match at Jerudong Park, there was a mad scramble—once a Bentley came into view—for everyone to "mount up" and all players to be at center field for the opening bowl in. It was already nearly an hour past the "scheduled" match time and I knew the hubbub was caused by whoever rode in that Bentley. Prince Jefri, certainly, word was that he loved his polo and never missed a match—and possibly the Sultan himself (then the richest man in the world). But nobody—including Alcides Campusano, the resident polo pro and manager of the entire horse operation—was ever sure whether The Sultan would show.

There were two grooms per horse in the pony tie lines and everyone had started moving at once, a beehive with a circling Bentley. Caught up in the excitement, I jumped on my first chukker mare, Suki, and raced out to midfield with the other players and umpires. Then there wasn't much to do but watch the Bentley continue its deliberate progress around the polo field, past the tie lines and up the backside of the grandstand where it disappeared from view. Seconds later, bedecked in boots and britches, Prince Jefri strode through a door at the bottom of the grandstands. Attendants handed him his tasseled helmet, a whip and mallet, and strapped on his kneepads. He was given a leg-up onto a glossy bay mare with no saddle pad and checkerboard brush strokes adorning the top of her butt. Prince Jefri and his mount jumped over the boards to where several polo balls had been strategically placed. He tapped one of these a couple of times with his white graphite mallet and galloped out to the throw-in where we waited at centerfield. His boots were the shiniest cordovan I had ever seen. "Good afternoon!" announced the Prince. And the ball was bowled-in.

So we were acquainted, at least technically, but we had never before held a private conversation.

"Yes?" From the cell phone pressed to my ear, emanates long-distance static and a disconcerting time delay. Can this really be him?

"I know you and other members of your family have played as our guests in Brunei. You come recommended to me."

Indeed, the curious accent could be Malay/British. It made sense. My father had played there years ago on a Myopia team, and possibly my brother Andrew as well. Recommended for what?

"Yes!! Thank you. How are you, Sir?"

I am distracted by the sight of my son scrapping for a ball on the soccer field. I am pleased that his coach is sitting on the bench and letting the kids play. It feels surreal to be having this conversation with a Malay royal at a rural South Carolina soccer park.

"You may be aware that I have had some issues with my brother and have lived on my own in London for some time."

It *is* him! Jefri's excesses—polo ponies, indiscreet parties, and a lavish luxury car collection—had become a sore spot for Brunei's Royal Family and the world press was on top of it. I recalled reading that Prince Jefri had been removed from his position as Finance Minister and had gone to live in the UK in a state of quasi-excommunication. But despite the concern for professional players of losing a big-spending patron, this bad publicity hadn't stopped Jefri's sons from playing on high-goal teams in England and Spain. It's him!

My strongest recollections from that first match back in 1990 were of sweltering heat and a lesson in etiquette. Halfway through the third chukker, our Citibank team was losing by a considerable *margin, the ball was teed-up for a Jerudong knock-in on the black (crude oil) backline[1] and I screamed to my teammates: "**I got Jefri!!**" He had proved a fast, attacking player and was extremely well-mounted. I couldn't really cover him anyway because of the horse difference—deep zone was my best shot—but I just wanted to clarify our coverage assignments. After the chukker, the pony-line beehive was humming as usual: grooms and horses everywhere, but here also white-coated waiters bustled around balancing silver trays with beaded glasses of ice water for half-time refreshment. I was slumped in a chair, dripping with sweat and pouring ice water over my head to find some relief from the pummeling heat, when an "envoy" sent from the grandstands found me.*

"Mr. Snow."

"Yes?"

*"Pleased to inform you to name His Royal Highness as **Prince Jefri** or, minimum, **Sir**, even when on the field of polo," the representative politely corrected me.*

It was so humid there were sweat spots blooming through my polo boots. "I understand. I'm sorry," I blurted out.

Last time I made that mistake.

"Yes, **Sir,** Prince Jefri. I had heard you moved to England. How can I help you?"

I watch my son and his teammates suck on Gatorades, trying to focus on this bizarre long-distance call, and speculate as to why this person had called *me*. But it doesn't take long for him to get to the point:

---

1 Most polo fields are marked (like football or soccer fields) with either lime or white paint. But in Brunei, the field markings (goal line; penalty lines of 30, 40, 60 yards; and a center T for throw-ins) are done with oil, the country's plentiful natural resource.

"How much do you pay for a polo pony in the United States?"

My mind races with the implications of this query. "That depends . . . ," I mumble, trying to buy time. *Get this one right, Adam.* "$50–60 thousand for a good horse and it could be much higher for top ones," I tell Prince Jefri.

There is a long pause. Is he testing me? He already knows what he wants to spend. I said too much? I said too little?

"You have a reputation for good horses. We have read about their accomplishments."

"Thank you."

"We have bought recently from New Zealand and Argentina, always a middleman is involved. And it has all gotten quite out-of-hand. I wish to buy direct. And I need someone I can trust. Do you have these horses for sale?"

At last, they have called the right person!

"Yes, Sir, I do. How many horses are you looking for?"

"I wish to buy forty 'top-class' ponies and transport to Brunei within a month. This must be handled with discretion. It is a birthday gift for my brother, The Sultan. Can you help us?"

I explain that if I could fill this order they would not all be from my personal string but that I will consider selling as many of my own as possible. For the rest I would act as an agent to purchase for him. *Can I find this number in such a short time?*

I beg for time. "Can you phone me in one hour, Sir? I would like to consult with my partner to confirm that I can fulfill your order." It occurs to me, too late, that I shouldn't let him off the phone.

But one hour later my cell phone rings again. This time I am in the Piggly Wiggly grocery store and the sense of disconnect is even more acute. In the hour or so since we had last spoken, I have called my wife, Shelley, for advice. She is game to help and recommends that we bring one more person into our partnership: Aiken neighbor and experienced horse seller Gabriel Crespo. The logistics of pulling off this deal in only thirty days, not to mention finding the air-transport into Brunei, are mindboggling. But if I express any doubts or reservations, Prince Jefri is likely to take his business elsewhere. And I don't want that. He has called the right person for the job and we stand a lot to gain from completing this transaction.

There are bags of Pork Cracklin' in my field of vision, as well as concern about being late to pick up my son at the soccer grounds, as I explain to Prince Jefri, "Yes, Sir, I can fill your order and provide forty 'top-class' horses in thirty days."

"Very good, Mr. Snow. Make sure they are 'top-class'."

And we're on.

To have any chance of fulfilling the Prince's "forty top-class" order in the matter of a month we have to move fast. By the time Shelley, Gabriel and I sit down in our home office to delegate responsibilities, we have generated some pretty good ideas: we will provide a digital PDF file with specifics on each horse including age, breeding (when known), feed, preferred playing bridle, and any known idiosyncrasies; Shelley will document her prepurchase exams on each of the top ponies we have committed to send; and, perhaps best of all, these horses will walk off the plane in Brunei wearing golden halters and lead-ropes in respect for the royal family which awaits them.

The three of us state our resolve to perform our end of this horse deal in an equitable manner. Indeed, the outcome will be something we can be proud of: sourcing, buying and shipping forty top ponies for top dollar. I have already begun trying horses, riding six ponies that morning on my lower field at New Haven

Farm. And Gabriel and I are working the phone lines to source quality ponies that can be bought. This is right up my alley! There are horse lists scribbled on legal pads: ones I have played, others we have seen, and some we have only heard second-hand are good. Six of these are my own horses. And then, for the remaining thirty-four, we can start trying/buying in Aiken and work out from there. And I enjoy the sense of *karma*—almost too good to be true—that my most recent personal horse acquisition (a nine-year-old gelding I purchased weeks prior to receiving Prince Jefri's call) already had the name, *Sultan*. A stout, easy chestnut, he will be the first horse in our package. And I let myself imagine him becoming The Sultan's personal favorite. This was going to work!

The next day we gather again for a status report and I wonder aloud how I should ask for the deposit. "Ask him how he wants to handle things," Gabriel coaches me. "He'll know what you mean. We should get a big one, 33–50 percent, before we start purchasing the horses." Our proposal is in: forty top-class horses will be provided with transport to Singapore (I couldn't find a horse carrier willing to fly to Brunei, and the Prince has agreed to this variation) within thirty days for $3.25 million. The price of air charter is high and—after some conference and discussion of precedents—I have padded the per-top-class-horse price to cover any unexpected expenses. But over the telephone Prince Jefri seems unfazed.

"How would you like to handle things, Sir?" I ask.

"We will transfer the funds into your account. Please e-mail me your bank information." I wasn't expecting the full amount all at once, but part of my preparation had involved opening a new Bank of America checking account (I deposited the "minimum balance" myself) so that all expenses related to this *Brunei 40 Deal* would be kept separate from our farm and polo operations. "Because of the time change, you will receive an SMS text message around 3:00 a.m.," the prince continued, "with an international number for the Isle of Wight where our offshore banking accounts are located."

I had wondered how these things happened. Now I knew. The Isle of Wight? I recalled a friend putting an unexpected windfall of cash (from a gambling trip with his polo patron) there once to avoid British taxes. I did the math for the time difference . . . and five or six hours ahead seemed about right. "Yes, Sir," I finally managed. "And I should call that number?"

"Call that number to finalize the deposit into your account."

I don't sleep much that night. Mostly I'm imagining all the horses that I will be trying over the next several weeks. When I go downstairs to check my phone in the wee hours of the morning, the number is on my text screen. I walk into the quiet of our home office, the same room we used to plan our course of action—I feel calm in here and I dial:

"Hello, *Royal Brunei Offshore Banking,* Dianne speaking." It is the voice of a British woman, maybe a bit stodgy, but then who can blame Dianne living on a remote island and dealing with this amount of money. She's probably paid to be tough. I can picture the trim office with a framed picture of The Sultan on the wall behind the administrator's staid desk.

"Yes, good morning. My name is Adam Snow. And I am calling at the request of Prince Jefri to coordinate payment for the forty polo ponies he has ordered."

"Yes, I was expecting your call. Please hold one moment."

I am still concerned about how big the invoice looks with us including the horse transport. ("Don't try to save your patron money," my first high-goal mentor had coached me years ago; but I have always found it difficult to shake my frugal Yankee roots.) Yet Prince Jefri insisted I package it all together . . . I assumed to keep it as a surprise for his brother.

"Sir?"

"Yes, Ma'am."

"I have the amount of 3.25 million USD here on my screen," Dianne tells me reading it off digit by digit. "Is that the correct amount?"

"Yes!" I say, perhaps a little too enthusiastically.

"For transfer to the Bank of America account ending in 0266. Correct?"

"Yes!" I can taste it landing in my bank account. It will be a mad scramble for the next month. But I'm up to the task. Of course, I am . . . they knew what they were doing when they chose me. *I will be using all of my honed skills . . . turning over every rock to find the next special horse. I love finding horses, sometimes I wonder whether this quest is even more compelling than playing the game. And partnering with Shelley will allow us to 'divide and conquer' the related tasks. The air carrier wants to fly out of Miami but if we can fly out of Atlanta and use the Olympic facilities for quarantine, it will be easier. Closer to us here in Aiken, South Carolina. I envision trailers crisscrossing the country laboring to collect these ponies and fill our order. Challenges are good.* She has the full amount on her screen; *and I appreciate the Prince's confidence in me to not mess with trivialities like partial deposits.* Her voice from the Isle of Wight brings me back from my reverie.

"Sir?"

"Yes?"

"When I press SEND TRANSFER, a window pops up indicating NO INSURANCE."

All I processed was that she actually had tried to press **Send!** *I have always wanted to fix up the eyesore, red clay-rimmed pond that is below our house: plant some bald cypress trees around its perimeter, keep the water level high (in spite of the cost of running the well), maybe have a fountain in the middle or a little stream running into one end. Fish . . . for sure. We will have it contoured properly with the help of a real pond architect! Then I can buy some horses of my own . . . top prospects that I will finish as champions! Likely, searching for these thirty-four will turn-up a pony (or several) which because they are ideally suited to me, I can ethically pull aside and find others to fill the order. And we should go ahead with that all-weather sport court for our kids—we had always thought we couldn't afford. But first there's this little technical glitch or something about insurance.*

"What about insurance?" I finally manage.

"An Insurance Guarantee Fee is required of the receiver to release funds from this account. This is standard procedure with Prince Jefri's expenditures; and will be refunded once the transaction is complete," Dianne explains.

Maybe they're just keeping tabs on him. But she actually did press Send!? "How much is it asking for?" I try.

"US$50,000," answers the voice from the Isle of Wight.

There is a long silence as I contemplate how to come up with this sum and fulfill the unexpected hiccup of "Prince Jefri's" *insurance guarantee fee.*

It took me days to fathom that I was the intended victim of a $50,000 scam. While I seriously considered the prospect of fulfilling this insurance "requirement" it was Shelley who put her foot down in no uncertain terms. **"You are not sending them one penny of our money!"** I had to admit that it did seem a bit strange that I would have to pay in order to sell some of my own horses. But my ego wouldn't allow me to accept that the whole thing had been a hoax. After all, I was the ideal person to handle such a large order in a professional and equitable manner. And—between my horse savvy, Gabriel's hustle, and Shelley's veterinary expertise and moral guidance—we were going to make a great team . . . really too good a team to let fold because of a small insurance requirement. And, in fact, a Royal Offshore banker had attempted to send the transfer.

Over the next ten days, I continued to call the *PJ* contact on my phone asking him to handle it or to pay me a small deposit of $50,000 that I would turn around and send to the Isle of Wight. *PJ* always answered my calls and adeptly dodged my creative proposals for him paying the insurance fee. If I left off calling for a day or two, he would phone me. And as the reality of a scam set in, I started asking increasingly difficult questions: "I know you played a lot with the Heguys. Can you tell me which brother died in a car accident?" "With which high-goal player is your son playing in Spain?" The answers for these questions were not on the tip of his tongue. One time, he feigned to have another call coming in and later called me back with the answer. Eventually he got defensive about being questioned for authenticity. "If you do not want our business, I will take it somewhere else." That gave me some pause. But I was now a nonbeliever. I dropped the *Sirs* and told him that I wasn't going to pay to provide my horses and service. Shelley even phoned him directly for one last try but it seemed like, from both ends, our deal was dead. Two weeks after I had received an order for forty horses I had to admit—with just an iota of doubt—that it had been an attempted fraud.

I telephoned the FBI to report the incident, but they didn't seem too interested and told me to call my senator. Someone in that office told me the calls probably originated in Nigeria, but I never knew for sure—they could have originated anywhere!—and I eventually gave up on my pursuit of law-enforcement.

Just now I dialed my *PJ* contact for the first time since 2009—011 44 7733 666025. Rather than an affected British/Malay accent, I was greeted with a female operator's voice: *the number you have dialed has been changed, disconnected or is no longer in service.* Even today, I harbor some belief that that could really have been him. I feel nostalgic about that contact and have no plans of deleting *PJ* from my phone. Perhaps that person will try me again at some point in the future. Or maybe an authentic Royal will call me from a different number with a prospective deal. In the meantime, if someone has a "forty top-class" horse order out there, we know how to make it happen! The forty golden halters are waiting . . .

CHAPTER 2

PLAYING AS A PRO

Polo is an esoteric sport that carries some baggage of privilege and that, especially in the U.S., most people don't even know can be played professionally. *Did you ever play with Prince Charles? But you're not Argentine? Yes,* I did. And *no,* I'm not.

There are disparate ways of making a living in and around the sport of polo: jobs such as team managers, horse trainers, horse brokers, grooms, umpires, club managers, farriers, veterinarians, and truck drivers are all available. All I ever wanted, however, was to be a professional player, someone whose predominant source of income was earned through tournament polo. Since polo is played on a pro-am basis,[2] with teams formed for just a single season or even just one tournament, the foundation of my career

---

2   Only in the Argentine Open do players get paid by corporate sponsors; see Chapter 13.

has been playing with and against a combination of professionals and amateurs on literally hundreds of different teams.

A professional polo player is somewhat akin to a travelling mercenary. In my busiest Palm Beach seasons, for example, I would be playing for several different teams during the same three-month period. A typical year might consist of the Florida season January through April, then travel to Australia, Malaysia or Brunei in the spring for a test match[3] or short tournament. A spring season in Aiken with a 16-goal team would be followed by a summer of high-goal polo in England, Santa Barbara or New York. The fall would find me playing a short stint in Aiken before heading to Argentina for the months of September through November. The first two weeks of December comprised my only real down time of the entire year, and they were spent preparing for the upcoming Florida season. To keep employed on such a consistent basis, I had to not only carry a high handicap, but also be considered "under-rated," (i.e., deemed to be playing above my handicap level.) I was also judged on my win-loss records, the quality of the horses I brought to the team, and my sportsmanship. Being a free agent, I was continually negotiating contracts and advocating for myself.

The handicapping system is what allows players of varying skill levels to fairly participate in the sport together[4]; it is an estimate of a player's value on the field to his/her team and is designed to promote an even playing field. Since it is a crucial element in understanding polo, it bears some explanation. The

---

3   A test match refers to an international friendly. For example, a U.S. team goes to Australia, and will be mounted by the hosts to play a match against a similarly rated Australian team. These events are often interesting from a cultural standpoint, but it's usually difficult for an entire team to get well-mounted on borrowed horses—a truly home field advantage.
4   Only the Argentine Open is truly open, with no handicapping.

word "goal" is somewhat confusingly applied after all handicaps and is loosely associated with that player's net worth in terms of both offense and defense over the duration of an average match. The four players' handicaps, in sum, is the rating of the team. The handicap scale ranges from –2 to 10, with 10 goals being the highest rating attainable (a 40-goal team carries the highest rating). Most "professionals" would be rated 4 goals and above. A player 7 goals or higher is among the top players of the world: as of 2014, the USPA (United States Polo Association) annual report indicates there were a total of 4,988 registered USPA members[5], with only thirty-nine players (fewer than 1 percent) carrying a handicap between 7 and 10 goals (during the years I was rated 10 goals, there were between five to eleven other 10-goalers in the world).

In its most common form, the pro-am model in polo consists of the team's player-owner (variably called an amateur, sponsor, or patrón) participating as a member of his or her four-person team while providing the salaries of the other three players (think John Henry getting to play in right field with his Boston Red Sox).[6] The sum of the four players' handicaps determines the level of tournament they wish to play—in a 16-goal tournament for example, the sum of the four players' handicaps cannot exceed sixteen goals. If the player-owner is rated 1 goal, he or she will hire up to fifteen goals worth of firepower to fill out the team (any combination such as 1, 7, 5, 3 or 1, 9, 4, 2 is possible; a team with a lower handicap is also permitted). Additionally,

---

5   All U.S. and international players must pay their annual membership fee (approximately $150) and obtain a proper USPA handicap in order to be eligible to participate in sanctioned U.S. tournaments.

6   There is little to no actual "prize money" in the sport. So teams are competing for the "trophy" and the pride that goes with it.

AMERICAN 10-GOALERS

Year	Name
1890	Foxhall P. Keene
1894	Rodolphe L. Agassiz
1894	John E. Cowdin
1894	Thomas Hitchcock
1900	Lawrence Waterbury
1902	James M. Waterbury Jr.
1917	Harry P. Whitney
1917	Devereux Milburn
1922	Thomas Hitchcock Jr.
1922	Louis E. Stoddard
1922	James Watson Webb
1925	Malcolm Stevenson
1934	Elmer J. Boeseke Jr.
1934	Cecil C. Smith
1937	D. Stewart B. Iglehart
1939	Michael G. Phipps
1982	Guillermo Gracida Jr.
1982	Thomas Wayman
1992	Owen Rinehart
1994	Michael V. Azzaro
2002	Adam Snow
2016	Pablo Pieres

the player-owner is responsible for paying the entry fee for the desired tournament, any club fees, and providing jerseys. Some teams will also provide horses, stabling or other benefits. The owner-player is literally a pro's "boss" in the sense that they write the checks. However, because of the bond that forms through being teammates in an intensely competitive environment, I have never thought of them as such. If handicaps act as the initial leveler, being teammates united for a common goal of winning a tournament completes the idea that "we are all in this together."

Professional players are generally contracted on a short-term basis—because tournaments only last one to four weeks, and players' handicaps change often, teams are forced to regroup constantly. Therefore professionals must spend a lot of time actively seeking jobs. Longer-term contracts, with the resultant job stability, are few and far between. I was extremely fortunate to have this situation during the first six years of my career, when I also had horses provided for me by my sponsor, Brook Johnson, who was a textiles entrepreneur and a former UNC basketball player. Brook had a passion for competitive sports and got exposed to polo through a clinic in England in 1985.[7] Although he was still green to the sport when we began playing together in 1987, he was a fierce competitor with his own goals for improvement. By the end of his first season of competitive polo, it was clear that Brook was hooked! After only one full year of tournament polo his handicap was raised from 0 to 1 goal (and he could finally quell his son's teasing chant: "Daddy's a zero! Daddy's a zero!"). Brook took pride in his defensive role at the #4 position and invested in quality ponies for himself and his team, CS Brooks. He went on to attain a very respectable 2-goal handicap and his team won many prestigious tournaments including the U.S. Gold Cup and the British Open.[8] As Brook quickly learned, the sport presents many compelling attractions

---

7   Major Dawnay is a famed Irish polo instructor who has made a successful career coaching and starting new players in the sport.

8   When the U.S. won the Westchester Cup (an international match between U.S. and U.K.) in 1992, Brook mounted over half of the American team with his horses. One of them, *Tormentosa*, played by Owen Rinehart, was honored with the Best Playing Pony prize on the day.

THE INS AND OUTS OF HANDICAPPING

All USPA handicaps are reevaluated twice each year by a volunteer committee comprised of both current and former players. This National Committee of about twenty-five members takes recommendations from its circuit (regional) representatives and ultimately determines which players need to be raised or lowered in this *relative* system intended to keep competitions balanced. Think golf handicaps, in reverse. At times, I have served on this committee myself and it is admittedly a challenging task. Unabashed lobbying by interested parties is a problem, especially since the nature of polo provides limited criteria on which to base objective decisions. If a team is very successful in one season, one or more of its team members may have their handicap raised for the subsequent one. In an effort to be maximally competitive, teams are proactive about seeking the hottest young talent and the most underrated players they can find (or hide). Sometimes a team may identify an improving, under-handicapped player and keep them out of tournament play for awhile, so as not to risk their handicap being raised before the one important event they wish to use him or her. Or, as I am sure happens in golf, too, there are situations where players, particularly those receiving a handicap in the U.S. for the first time, may sandbag for a game or two when they know they are being observed. But those individuals may be available for only one season at their current handicap anyway. I had one experience where my team had contracted with a promising young player only to have to scramble last minute and find a new one because his handicap was unexpectedly raised midseason. This so-called Monster Rule allows for a player's handicap to be shifted two goals at any point in the year if deemed grossly underrated; it is intended to prevent ringers from sneaking in under the Handicap Committee's radar.

for amateur sponsors: working towards successful partnerships with horses, a team dynamic, exciting athletic competition on into middle age, physical exertion, speed, danger and—perhaps most intriguing—a way to forget the worries of the office.

After the 1994 season in England, I was gently "made redundant" for the subsequent summer by CS Brooks (we hadn't won a

CS Brooks winning 1991 Challenge Cup, Palm Beach Polo. Andrew Snow, Adam Snow, Owen Rinehart, Brook Johnson.

major tournament), and it hit me hard. I had gotten accustomed to playing high-goal polo at least two seasons of every year for an organization that fully supported me with horses. It had provided me a wonderful start. Now I was on my own. But I was familiar with cold-calling; I had always worked hard on the phone and fax lines (in the days before e-mail and Facebook), literally drumming up interest for creating teams—and jobs for myself in the seasons I wasn't playing with CS Brooks. Out of necessity, I embraced my new free agency as a means to avoid getting complacent. Since

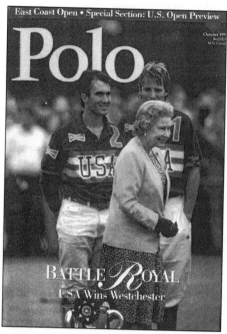

USA Westchester Cup victory, Guards Polo Club, England, July 1992.

I could no longer count on consistent work, I needed to be playing at the top of my handicap range to ensure that invitations for the upcoming season would come my way. I needed to improve my string of horses. I needed to *up my game.* If I played well enough, I could maybe even have the possibility of picking and choosing between more than one offer. If not, the alternative was unemployment. My task was to stay focused on playing well and winning while not becoming unmoored by the inherent flux of the job market.

Throughout this nomadic and uncertain career, Shelley and I were often living in different states and even on different continents, and she was mostly responsible for raising three children and managing the behemoth that was my polo operation (a farm, multiple employees, and up to forty horses). Our life with and on horses proved both the point of our focus and the glue that kept us together. While my passion was winning the next game, Shelley's passion was improving the lives of the animals that played it. I deferred to her for the frequent tough calls back at the barn (when **not** to play a horse, for example.)

HIGH-GOAL POLO

The player-owner with the means and desire to play the high-goal winter season in Palm Beach, Florida, is entering the big time and will be competing against the most serious, established pro-am polo teams in the world. At this level, they will need to hire from amongst the relatively small pool of world-class professionals in order to raise their collective team handicap to 20 goals (the current January and February tournament levels) or 26 goals (the current level of the U.S. Open, and its' precursors, in March and April). Because it is so large and multilayered, at this level a "team" is better understood as an "organization," and can include farms, polo fields, trucks, trailers, large numbers of horses, and many employees including managers, grooms, veterinarians, as well as polo players. A handful of teams with sufficient budgets play year-round in different venues and countries. Polo tends to migrate with the sun, following latitudes according to the season, and going where the climate is suited to running horses and green grass.

She handled these decisions of balancing a horse's health with my polo objectives with equanimity, weighing the short-term versus long-term implications—and she hardly ever put a foot wrong. Above and beyond her healing hands and veterinary skills, she was the adviser, rider, confidante, and horse trainer I needed. Our partnership was vital to my success as a professional polo player.

Although on more than one occasion I considered shifting to a different career with a more consistent source of income and fewer expenses, the rewards of sticking with professional polo have been profound. I get to work outside. I love the feel of horses under me, as well as the constant challenge of maintaining and improving their on-field performance. There is longevity, relative to other sports, because the horses are my legs for getting around the field. There is the stimulus of playing with different combinations of players; there is the chance of getting to know them, through a common objective, as people as well as teammates. And one of my initial attractions to the sport—travelling around the country and world—still has not

STARTING OUT

Today, the opportunities for a young professional to be mounted by a team are few and far between. When I first arrived in Florida in 1988, there were probably a half-dozen organizations that mounted their professionals; in the 2015 U.S. Open, there were only two such teams. The challenge for a young, aspiring professional today is that the all-in sacrifice of owning and maintaining horses, as well as working diligently on improving as a player, are requirements for having any chance of getting paid offers to play. But even that doesn't guarantee anything. With a finite number of teams competing in any given tournament, it is possible that no teams will require your handicap for that particular season. With mandatory equipment consisting not only of boots, helmet, kneepads and mallets, but often also a truck and trailer and a minimum of eight horses with their requisite tack, this outlay is what makes the sport seemingly inaccessible for most. Lower goal players struggle to make ends meet with the high expenses incurred, and will often have to supplement their income with horse sales, and managerial or umpiring side jobs. But polo is a passion project, and many make their living in its world.

gotten old. Beyond all else, however, it is the competition, the raw basic feelings of intensity of playing a sport something like ice-hockey-on-horses, running around at speeds of up to thirty mph, that I am addicted to. It makes me feel alive. Yes, there is such a thing as a professional polo player, and I count myself as one of the fortunate few to lay claim to it.

CHAPTER 3

THE POLO PONY:
THE HORSE IN THE GAME

Not only humans play the game of polo—one of the most salient aspects of the sport is that it is played on horseback. Behind that simple fact lies an entire world—of breeding, training, caring for, conditioning, and feeding these amazing equine athletes. The key to winning lies in accomplishing the endless work and building the vast knowledge and skill sets required to show up to the field with eight horses ready to play a game. The best team tactics and most skilled ball-handling ability of the player are worthless if he/she can't *get there;* arriving at precisely the right time and place on a field which is 300 yards by 160 yards is the job of the seasoned polo pony,[9] each and every seven-and a-half minute chukker of its life.

---

9   In polo, it is common to use the terms pony (technically an equine under 14.2 hands, where a hand equals 4 inches) and horse interchangeably, without any regard for their height.

Imagine preparing not only yourself for the finals of the U.S. Open, but readying eight other sentient athletes as well. And they can't tell you if they need more work, a spell of rest in the pasture, or where they might feel soreness. Yet, preparing them to perform at their best—getting the feed and exercise right, the injuries diagnosed and healed, settling on the tack and bit selections so that both horse and rider feel comfortable—is easily as important as the human player's preparation. Here is where the sport gets complicated.

Horses are painstakingly schooled to learn the game, and the best surely intuit what it takes to win plays. Comprised of mostly thoroughbreds, world-class polo ponies demonstrate an amazing range of athleticism: they run flat out at speeds up to 40 mph, stop on a dime, turn inside out, and ride-off other horses. And all of these skills must be performed in a steady enough manner to allow the rider to hit a bouncing three-inch diameter ball. Polo's best human athletes acknowledge that the horse is "up to 80 percent of the game"; therefore, the pursuit of excellence in polo goes hand-in-hand with the cultivation of exceptional horses.

A polo pony playing at a high level in the sport must be extremely well-conditioned; in fact, it is among the fittest of equine athletes, for the horse must not only have the ability to run at top speed (around 35 mph) for the length of the field, sometimes several times during a chukker, but also make lots of sudden stops, bursting starts, and seemingly impossible changes of direction. Games vary, but on average a horse will travel a few miles during its playing time on the field. To achieve this level of fitness and agility requires horsemanship, time, and hard work; but the saving grace is that these movements are entirely natural to horses. Watching horses cavort and frolic in a field you will see all the moves necessary on the polo field; what changes is only that a rider is directing them.

When a high-goal team shows up for a game, they are responsible for bringing up to forty horses to the field. Each player brings a trailer with his/her mounts (usually eight-ten), and two to three grooms will be working to prepare the horses before the game, hold spares, and cool out the ponies after they've played. The logistics are tremendous, and that's just game day. If you are a professional player and are responsible for mounting yourself for tournament play, your entire life becomes subsumed by the need to maintain a string of ponies that allows you to play your best. The organization of this machine is inextricably linked with your success.

While the life of a polo pony can be hard, much has been done to align the welfare of the animals with the goals of the game in recent years. In many ways, polo ponies have it good. They are allowed to be social—an important aspect of happiness in this herd-bound species—for they live, exercise, and travel in groups. The physical demands of the sport are in line with their natural proclivities. And they often get prolonged periods of down time on pasture between seasons. These factors translate to happy horses. Polo ponies also usually receive excellent medical care, for, even if not every single owner has a deep bond to each of their horses, they are valuable assets.

The story of one of our mares,[10] Rio, highlights the significance of the horse in the game of polo, as well as the complexity

---

10 A mare is an adult female horse; in high-goal polo the vast majority of successful ponies are female. Mares possess the competitiveness and drive lacking in most geldings and the levelheadedness hard to come by in a stallion.

of the modern game. She is an excellent prototype of the modern polo pony, and to do the tale justice, it is best to start with her mother, Riojana.

Adam first met Riojana when he travelled to Argentina in the fall of 1990 to play in the Camara Diputados, a 30-goal tournament. His teammate and mentor, Alfonso Pieres, generously provided him a string of young horses and thus supported Adam's effort to improve his polo. Riojana was in that group, and quickly became Adam's favorite. She was a bay mare, with a little bit of an ugly head, but pretty doesn't matter when you have power and quickness. Alfonso was able to sell Riojana following that tournament to his (and Adam's) patron, and she first went to the U.S. to play and then on to England. Adam's handicap kept rising over the summers in England, when she was reliably his best horse. Her strength was her lateral movement at speed, and plenty of speed at that. However, in the summer of 1992, after being an instrumental part of USA's victory over England in the Westchester Cup[11], Riojana underwent surgery for a lingering ankle injury at Newmarket Equine Hospital in England. Although pasture sound, she never recovered sufficiently to play polo again.

Riojana travelled to Wyoming to have a second career as a broodmare on a ranch that had been breeding polo ponies for decades. Adam negotiated a deal with the owner that in exchange for giving them the mare, he had right of first refusal, at fair market value, on all her offspring. Riojana's first foal, a filly, he bought at age two and dubbed her Rio. She was the same color and build as her mom, but a little bigger due to her American thoroughbred father. Riojana continued to be a prolific mother,

---

11 A traditional competition between the two countries.

BUT THE GOOD ONES COME ALL WAYS

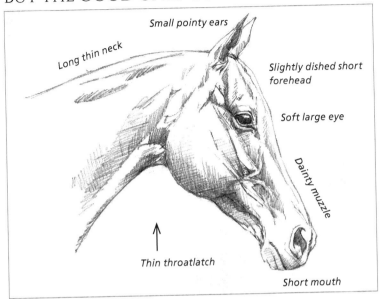

Small pointy ears

Long thin neck

Slightly dished short forehead

Soft large eye

Dainty muzzle

Thin throatlatch

Short mouth

CONVENTIONALLY PRETTY

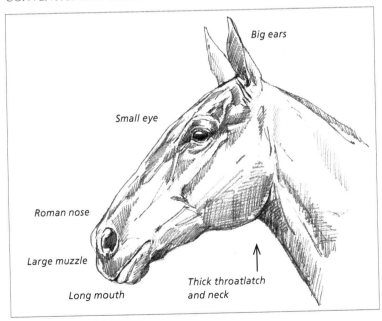

Big ears

Small eye

Roman nose

Large muzzle

Long mouth

Thick throatlatch and neck

CONVENTIONALLY UGLY

in total having ten foals, all of who played polo. When the Wyoming ranch owner passed away, we brought Riojana back to Aiken. She lived in contented retirement to age thirty-two, a testament to her tremendous physical vitality.

Rio was trained over the course of several years, was always an "easy keeper", and she took to polo right off. By age five, she was playing in tournament polo, and Adam was getting excited about her. I remember Mark Bryan, who was working with us at the time training horses, saying about her "this mare will take Adam to 10 goals." He ended up being right! Rio starred in a PBS documentary titled *Horse & Rider*, and was a stalwart on many of Adam's best lists, travelling all across the country to compete and even to Argentina in 2004 to play in the Open there.[12] She had sufficient speed and power but her strength was always her handle, which translates as her maneuverability in the short plays.

When she suffered a tendon injury in the spring of 2005, she became a new poster child—this time for a novel therapeutic treatment involving stem cells. When she returned to full fitness the following year, her picture was splashed across magazines advertising the success of the treatment.

Rio retired in 2015, and now it is her turn to begin a second career as a mother. She won't have a chance to be as multiparous as her mother—good general care as well as advanced veterinary technology prolonged her playing career until she was nineteen years old. Regardless of whether she gets pregnant or not, she will enjoy the green pastures and her friends she's had all her

---

12 Our horses travel around the U.S. in a twelve-horse trailer; Rio flew with other horses in a cargo plane to and from Argentina.

life in the comfort of what has always been her home—our farm in Aiken, South Carolina. Hopefully the circle continues and another brown filly will be born sometime in the upcoming years, and we'll have to think up a name to continue the line of polo prowess and performance passing along the maternal line.

Yoko, Pumbaa and Bag Lady flying to England for 1999 summer season.

CHAPTER 4

A CAREER FOR LIFE

The prospects for retirement aren't good. It is said that polo players will "go down swinging" due to their propensity for using their last penny to finance their avocation/vocation. Others will take their last breath on the backs of their horses, either through unfortunate accident or by a medical event which could have occurred anywhere, anytime, but happily enough for them, occurred on the back of their favorite mount. Polo is a game that people start playing. They rarely make the willful decision to stop.

So it was for Adam. As college graduation and the presumed end of competitive team sports approached, his mother worried about how he would cope without the adrenaline of his "next game." She remembered him as an eleven-year-old "squirt" hockey player imaging goals in the foyer mirror as he waited for his ride to the rink. Small round objects, and the various physics involved in their movement, were clearly an obsession from an early age. One story Adam's father remembers is that at age two Adam was obsessed with a simple game of kicking a ball into a washtub, and begged everyone around him to play constantly. In college it was lacrosse and hockey—and polo during the summer—that took on lives of their own. In his twenties, athletics still brought a focus and ritual to his life that would be hard to replace. So instead of facing a lifestyle switch and pursuing a "grown-up career," he turned his energies to the one sport he stood a chance of playing professionally beyond college—polo. As a 4-goal player when he graduated in 1987, he articulated his rationale for setting off to Argentina: "to travel, learn a new language, and see if I can get good enough to play one winter professionally in Florida." *One winter* implied his motivation was more "walkabout"[13] than vocation; it also provided cushion should he prove not "good enough." So he followed the adrenaline, not consciously—because he had downplayed his mother's concerns about it being a hard thing to leave—but instinctively.

Even bodily injury didn't deter Adam from his career path in polo. His high-flying first season in Wellington, Florida[14] came to an abrupt halt when, during his second-ever 26-goal game, he got hit behind the saddle by an opponent while at a full gallop. His horse went down, and he lay unconscious on the ground for several seconds. After the ambulance ride, and the assessment at Wellington Regional Hospital, he found he had a broken right collarbone and a dislocated left thumb (in those days there was

---

13 An Australian term for taking time off as a young adult to see the world.
14 The undisputed polo capital of the U.S.

no mention of the concussion!), which would keep him out of action for at least six weeks.

At the time, he had no health insurance. Recent college graduates—especially ones with student loans still to be paid off—don't always think of these things. And, even if he had, it is unlikely any companies would have wanted to insure a twenty-three-year-old freelance polo player. He appealed to his former team. They allowed him to keep driving the Jeep they had loaned him for the season but, since they had already paid his salary, they declined helping with any medical expenses. He couldn't really blame them; it wasn't like he was playing for the Boston Bruins, protected by a player's union. So he spent the entirety of his meager first-season earnings on a cast, a sling, a figure-eight strap for his clavicle, and the good care he had received in the hospital.

Adam's season was over. He watched a game or two, but he'd never liked being a spectator, and there really wasn't much for him to do in Florida anymore. A week after the accident, he was back living at his mom's apartment in Cambridge, Massachusetts, where he found work bussing tables at a Mexican restaurant in Harvard Square. During the job interview, the manager looked at Adam funny when he noticed the cast on Adam's left wrist, but Adam demonstrated that he could still carry the large trays. In fact, it provided good support—kind of like a kickstand—and he got the job. For two months, with only the vague prospect of a polo job on the horizon, Adam ferried plates of catfish and *arroz con frijoles* back and forth between the kitchen and the busy tables of The Border Cafe. He got skilled enough that he could carry two trays at one time. And he could carve out two-day windows here and there to visit Shelley (now a college junior) in

New Haven, Connecticut. By the time his body healed, Adam's next playing job had solidified, and in June he returned to the polo circuit and recommenced playing, this time on a 20-goal team (CS Brooks) in Greenwich, Connecticut.

Adam proved to be an exceptional talent. Rated at 6-goals, he was one of only a handful of Americans considered to be a "high-goal" player—and he was still young, and presumably on an upward trajectory. But in December 1988, faced with my imminent graduation and expected move to Hong Kong for a two-year teaching fellowship, he decided to quit polo and follow me. At twenty-five years old, his "walkabout" was over, and he vowed to put down his mallet and get a "real" job after his commitments in Florida (January and February) and Connecticut (June and July) were met. Adam and I got married on June 3, 1989, one week after my Yale graduation, and we headed off (albeit separately—which should have been a warning sign!) on our new adventure.

Upon arrival in Shatin, Hong Kong, Adam hit the ground running. He had a job with the textiles company of his polo sponsor (warning sign #2?) and so he immediately purchased two suits, a briefcase, and a fax machine, and made frequent visits to the American Chamber of Commerce to learn his new trade. The stage was set for a successful change of career path. It lasted two weeks. One day, I came home from my teaching job at the Chinese University of Hong Kong to find my husband standing on a chair in our tiny Hong Kong apartment bouncing tennis balls off the wall with his polo mallet. When a polo friend called that week from Auckland, New Zealand, and heard my story, he laughed. "Send him down to me!" he quipped. A week later Adam left Hong Kong for another island—the North Island of New Zealand—and was back on a horse swinging his mallet at real polo balls on real grass fields. The textiles job transmuted back into a polo job for the next summer in England, and all talk of an alternate career was shelved.

As Adam focused on playing polo professionally out of college and accrued tournament experience, his handicap kept rising, reflecting his talent and commitment. However, when he was raised to 7 goals on January 1, 1990, he was officially residing in Hong Kong with me. He didn't own any horses, and he was living in a country that didn't have a single polo field. But resourcefulness has always been one of Adam's strengths, and he spread the word that he wanted to travel for paid opportunities in the region. At 7 goals, he was one of the highest-rated players in Asia so invitations started to come. This combination of travel and playing polo while getting paid was intoxicating. His wanderlust was only somewhat dampened by the fact that I could not travel freely with him. We still however managed to hike around Tongariro National Park in New Zealand, bunker in a Manila hotel during a foiled coup attempt against President Corazon Aquino of the Philippines, float through stilt villages in the rivers near Bandar Seri Begawan in Brunei, and dive into the South Pacific off Bondi Beach in Sydney, Australia.

In 1991, Adam wrote a piece for the Myopia Polo Program describing these experiences, as well as the polo games he had played and the polo people he had met during the previous year. I found the typewritten pages buried in his files as I was searching for something else in the course of writing this book. It represents Adam's attempt to explain (to members of his hometown club) what he was actually doing with his life, at a time when being a professional polo player was a relatively new concept. Rereading it, I was struck by how it captured the spirit of adventure Adam was seeking at that time, as well as the joy in the travel he undertook. He embodied the philosophy of *have boots, will travel.* The article is also a reminder to me that from the very beginning, Adam's polo life consisted of *writing it down.* He lived, he played, he wrote; he made a way for it all to work regardless of his locale or circumstances.

Adam plays for Team USA at the Royal Easter Show, Sydney, Australia.

The summer found him playing in England for his polo sponsor (all talk of sourcing greige goods long forgotten), and from his first season in Cowdray Park, his career snowballed. He continued winning tournaments and going up in handicap. It was exciting for him, the life of a professional athlete. He unexpectedly found he was earning decent money, too—enough to pay off his student loans and buy twenty-four acres of farmland in Aiken, South Carolina.[15]

Thus followed a decades-long career of professional polo. Adam's passion for the sport sustained him through years of

---

15 Aiken has a long history of polo and equestrian activity, and its climate and soil favor horses.

travelling all over the globe. His career was very solid; job offers were continuous, and he often got to pick and choose which teams to play on. He won numerous tournaments, and was finally rewarded—after a year in 2002 when he won almost everything he played in—with a 10 handicap. He had said earlier in his career that he would like to quit while on top, but after a few years at 10-goals, when he got demoted to 9, that sentiment seemed to vanish. The idea of choosing to put the sport down was unimaginable to him.

The ease of continuing to play polo professionally well past one's youth is enabled by the partnership with equine mounts, who, let's face it, do most of the physical work. A poloist must maintain strength and flexibility, but the natural decline of cardiovascular capability with age is a nonissue. And of course the mind only gets sharper with more experience in the game. In addition to being your legs and heart the horses also provide a compelling attraction—it is hard to escape the pull they exert. A life of spending hours outside riding horses, with the next tournament always on the horizon, keeps one coming back for more. So even after attaining his objective of a 10-goal handicap, Adam's single-mindedness was simply transmuted:

In 2006, my handicap started to decline and my new pursuit became experiencing the surge I got from playing my best. In her short story about a bull-rider, Annie Proulx describes it as 'that blazing feeling of real existence.'

In one's forties a professional athlete may be foolish not to start questioning one's longevity in their chosen sport. Adam's mentor, Alfonso Pieres, had advised him about ageing gracefully: "Don't fight the natural handicap decline." This proved to be good advice, for each year Adam went down in handicap, he had great opportunities to play, and continued to win tournaments. By taking good care of himself and being smart about his team choices, Adam was able to continue to avoid the inevitable.

But getting old isn't easy for anyone, much less someone who makes their living by their agility, hand-eye, and coordination. In 2009, Adam remembers:

> *Some of my strengths—like quickness—weren't as pronounced. One 26-goal game, a young Argentine hot-shot, Sapo Caset, shot by me to score a goal—and I was on my best horse! When I called Shelley that night to commiserate, she responded, "Honey, they're half your age out there." It was the new reality. And getting the yips about taking 30-yard penalties became a problem—and a source of family jokes.*

In spite of struggling to keep up with the speed of the game—or maybe because of it, as he redoubled his work—his team reached the finals of the U.S. Open and in that match he won MVP. 2009 ended up being the last U.S. Open he was ever to play; in that tournament, he did "go out on top."

Despite his continued successes on the field, Adam started to feel that "continuing to skip around to every polo opportunity that presented itself would likely end in a broken marriage and little connection with his children." I was certainly at my wits end with his being gone so many months of the year, and was pressuring him to be home more. Adam also realized that he needed to parcel out his energies a little better, and get more physical and mental rest, so he started not accepting every single offer to play. For the first time in the quarter-century of his career, he felt that he had more to lose than to gain by continuing to seek employment for every spare week, season after season. Winning another tournament no longer seemed like the do-or-die situation it once had. Maybe there wasn't that much more to prove? The winter of 2012 he turned down a good offer in order to stay home. He reasoned his eldest son was soon going to be leaving for college, and he wanted to be more a part of his family. Summer, however, brought him to an exciting season of 20-goal polo in Santa Barbara, California. As a result of this successful season (you are always only as good as your last game!), he got an offer to play the following winter in Florida, and took it.

While Adam was living alone in Wellington in January and February of 2013, he was pretty miserable. He had everything that had heretofore been his *raison d'etre*—a great team, Florida competition, his best horses—but all he wanted was to be home in Aiken. Maybe the more than two decades of unrelenting mental pressure, physical stress, and extended times alone had taken their toll. So Adam made a decision that spring—he was going to retire. When his friend Roderick Vere Nicoll got wind of these thoughts, he asked Adam to write a piece for the British polo magazine he published, *Hurlingham*, about his resolution. Soon the backpedaling began:

> "It's not exactly retirement," Adam qualified over the phone.
> "Well, whatever you want to call it, will you write a story about it?" Roderick asked.
> "Yes," he decided.

The process of writing this article—eventually published as "The Seven Ages of Polo"—caused Adam untold consternation, for he had to figure out what exactly he was doing before he publicized it. Was he truly retiring? Through the painstaking endeavor of getting his confused thoughts on paper, he came to realize that he didn't want to sell all his horses, which would be the first condition of proper *retirement*. He also eventually came to the conclusion that he didn't want to quit polo entirely—what else was there for him *to do*? What he *did* want was to get off the proverbial treadmill: he wanted to stop going blindly from one season to the next; stop being always on the move; stop always being on the lookout for the next job. At age forty-nine Adam was searching for a balance between his personal and professional lives. So he took an intermediate step—he called a high-goal patron and initiated the process of selling one of his best mares. This was the first time he had ever parted with a favorite playing pony.[16] This transaction proved that at least from a financial perspective, he didn't need to continue making a salary as a player to make a living.

In August 2013, as Adam was painstakingly writing draft after draft of his *Hurlingham* article while playing in Santa Barbara, our oldest son Dylan departed for his first year of college. I texted Adam a photo of our three sons hugging an emotional goodbye in our home's foyer in Aiken, and it hit him—in addition to his guilt at not being present for this landmark—that this gang wasn't going to be around forever. And, if Adam had regrets that his mind (and often body) were elsewhere during much of Dylan's childhood, it didn't mean he had to make the

---

16 Tula went on to play to great acclaim in both the US and Argentine Opens.

same mistake with his two younger sons, while they were still around. He summarized these new thoughts:

> *Today, being on the farm—caring for our horses, our children, and our house, training young horses, and mentoring the young players who pass through Aiken on the Team USPA program—feels productive. Being away for long seasons on my own—even with the 'blazing' feeling of playing—does not.*

As the Pacific Coast Open games ticked by, Adam wrote in his *Hurlingham* article that he would "continue to play when it fits with my new objective of playing quality polo, not quantity." He eventually came up with the following definition for his *partial* retirement: "I am retiring from high-goal polo—at least long high-goal seasons—during the months when my kids are in school." Basically, this meant that his only "retirement" was from the Florida winter season. Adam continues to enjoy the game and lights up like a little boy in a candy shop when he gets new opportunities to play. In the last few years he has played competitive fall and spring seasons in Aiken, summer polo in California and Wyoming, and the odd international test match. So even in his fifties, the prospects for Adam's retirement aren't good.

CHAPTER 5

ACHIEVING 10: WHY ME?

A top player asked me one time how I ever made it to 10 goals. He wasn't questioning my ability, but rather wondering about my unorthodox path. He knew for example that I was born in Japan, grew up only playing summer vacations, and chose ice hockey and lacrosse in college, even though my school had a polo team. And then once I started as a pro, I didn't even own my first horse until I was 7 goals. He had a point.

But it wasn't as if I started from scratch. I grew up in a town with a polo club, Hamilton, Massachusetts, and most of my father's side of the family played so I was exposed to the sport at a young age.[17] My earliest riding memories—not fond—are

---

17 My dad started in his early twenties when his half-brother, Donald Little, initiated the rebirth of polo at Myopia Hunt Club. On his stint with the Strategic Air Command in Arizona, Don was invited to try "cowboy polo," and fell in love with the sport. He and his wife, Judy Little, returned to Ipswich, Massachusetts in 1958 towing a self-fashioned horse trailer, two quarter horse polo ponies, and a passion to rekindle interest in a sport which had not been played locally since before WWII. At the time of this writing, polo continues to thrive at Myopia.

of Dad requiring my help exercising his four horses on frosty mornings before he left for work. My grandfather, a career pilot, gave me my first stick and ball lessons and lectured me on the aerodynamics of a good polo swing. I admired my older cousin's skills in hitting the ball at a gallop. But, when I was prodded to enter my first family practice at age ten, I fell off the loaned horse, Scooter, three times and refused to get back on.[18] Over a year later, my dad pushed me to give the sport another try: "You have the opportunity I never had—to get really good, by starting so young." But it wasn't until I entered a kids' clinic at age twelve, and began competing with my peers to score a goal, that any residual fears of the scary beast under me were forgotten.

That same summer I recall observing the first travelling "pro" and highest rated player I had ever seen competing in a Myopia[19] tournament. His name was Benny Gutiérrez, he was a "7-goaler" and I studied his every move. For months afterwards, my brothers and I pedaled around the paved circle in front of our house playing bike polo, battling to keep the ball away from each other, and commentating on our stick-work like play-by-play announcers—"Benny, Benny, Benny Gutiérrez goes to goal!"

I juggled the polo ball on my little mallet and pretended that the number of consecutive hits would determine my eventual highest handicap. In those days, the highest-rated local player was 4 goals, and I was content with four taps in the air. The first time I got to hit on a wooden-horse, I didn't get down until my

---

18 Uncle Donald leant me the horse and I think he might have been trying to sell him to Dad. The first time I got dumped, Scooter gave a little crow-hop. The next two times I was so scared that I pretty much bailed whenever I received the ball. When I refused to get on after my third spill, Uncle Donald climbed on Scooter "to line him out." An empty feedbag blew across the field, Scooter cut in two, and my uncle got dumped, too.

19 Myopia Hunt Club in Hamilton, Massachusetts is the club where I learned to play polo.

hands were blistered.[20] I always wanted to practice with a ball. By the time I reached high school, Myopia was hosting the East Coast Open, one of the best summer tournaments in the country. Nobody told me to do it, but even before I was good enough to get invitations to play, I was watching and copying the high-goal players who participated in this event. I was learning.

I played polo like every other sport I was exposed to, with a full-on commitment. Whatever the season—hockey, polo, baseball, basketball, lacrosse, football, tennis—I could be found shooting lead-filled pucks in the garage, whipping the lacrosse ball against a chicken-wire backstop outside our house, or serving buckets of balls to an imaginary opponent on a nearby court. I assumed that I was not as naturally gifted as those I competed against. I'm not sure where this attitude came from—perhaps returning from Japan in 5th grade I feared I was behind my peers in organized sports, or it could have been my insecurity for being small for my age—but I trusted that working harder than everyone else was the way to bridge this perceived gap.

The long hours of practice did not mean that I excelled at all of these sports. As the back-up quarterback on a hapless high-school football team, I started only one game, this because our coach got so angry with the starting quarterback—for messing around on the bus ride to an away game—that he decided to bench him. I can still picture Coach Blake wending his way back through the aisle to where I sat: "Snow, you're starting at QB today." And the butterflies in my stomach began to soar. When I leaned in to

---

20   Just what it sounds like, a wooden horse is a training tool for hitting a lot of balls without tiring a live animal. It is usually built in a cage with sloped flooring that allows the balls to roll back to within hitting distance. This incident happened in 1973 in Kuala Lumpur, Malaysia—while our family was returning from my father's two-and-a-half year posting as a foreign correspondent for the Boston Globe in Tokyo. I was nine years old.

take the first snap, I could barely see over my squatting linemen. I went three-and-out for the loss of a yard or two and we punted on fourth down. At least no turnovers! By our team's next possession, Coach had reconciled his differences with the usual starter and I was back on the bench where I belonged.

Even for sports I played well, I was a classic late bloomer. I played ice hockey and lacrosse in college but my rise was of the "slow and steady" variety. While in high school I hadn't even made these sports' varsity teams until my junior year. "Cream always rises to the top," my lacrosse coach penned beside my name on the stat sheet he posted on our locker room bulletin board.[21] It was my senior year at St. Paul's in Concord, New Hampshire and I listed somewhere in the middle of the pack for the league's top scorers. Motivated by Coach's words, I did rise to the top of the Independent School League in goals and assists by the end of the season. I received a limited amount of college recruitment as an attackman in lacrosse—one school gave me a stick—but playing college hockey was my dream. My dad had played in college, and I grew up believing that this was what I wanted (whether from him or from me, I've never been sure). I was still small by my senior year of high school. Although I was a decent player, I centered the second line and I wasn't leading the team—let alone the league—in anything.

So I deferred college for a year and went to Sweden to play four months of an appropriate level of hockey in order to "let

---

21 Cliff Gillespie was an ex-Marine sergeant, chemistry teacher, and long-time coach of the lacrosse team at St. Paul's School in Concord, New Hampshire. He famously required his squad to run a two-and-a-half mile "loop" through the woods every day before practice—in boots! We polished our cleats before each and every match, and were never ever late for a team commitment. He put the fear of God in us, and we idolized him. Cliff coached multiple undefeated seasons, including my junior and senior years (1981–82).

myself grow."[22] I felt it was my only real shot of walking-on the DI college team. And besides, it represented a cultural learning experience even if my hockey aspirations did not pan out. Once at Yale, I battled to make varsity hockey—worked as hard as I could in dry-land training, lifted weights with the team—and, even when I was selected for JV, I kept working. Later in the season, the team had some injuries and I was called up to dress for two games. By sophomore year I was firmly on the varsity squad, and as a senior I was elected captain and played first-line right wing beside a center who went on to play a long, successful career in the NHL.[23] It just seemed that the longer I worked on things, the better I got. When it came to considering polo as a potential career after college, this became a source of confidence.

93rd Eli Captain, Adam Snow

1986-87 Yale Men's Hockey

Plenty of college ice-time.

---

22 My Swedish stepmother, Lena Granberg, found me this opportunity. A friend of hers was a hockey coach, who offered me to play at his club GIK (Goteborg Ishockey Club). And Lena's relatives, Ulf and Marta Schele, graciously hosted me at their home.

23 Bob Kudelski played for the Los Angeles Kings, the Ottawa Senators, and the Florida Panthers during his nine-year NHL career. In 1994 he was selected to play in the NHL All-Star game, where he scored two goals. Not a bad college linemate!

By the time I graduated from college at twenty-three years old in 1987, I was rated 4 goals and I began playing polo full time. I had my work ethic and also the benefit of all the other sports training. Some transferable lessons consisted of how to eat, sleep, establish a pre-game routine, practice imagery, position myself on defense, and get open for a pass. And for the first time in my life, I was focused on just one sport.[24]

I relished the travel and cultural experiences that polo afforded me, but I never played polo for the lifestyle. The image popular media tends to portray—glamorous and steeped in upper-crust privilege—always made me squirm. I understood this depiction as a double-edged sword: it brought luxury product sponsorship, and therefore money, to the sport but it also turned off much of the general public who could not get beyond this image to appreciate the real sport. I felt far more comfortable in the barn—mucking, exercising, icing, cleaning tack or repairing mallets—than in almost any social setting related to the sport. When I played in front of the hoopla of big hats, champagne half-times, and tailgate contests it felt like something apart from my life in the sport. Even before I turned pro, a trophy presentation in front of the stands often followed a Sunday match, and involved signing a ball for a child or receiving a silver-plated trophy for a win. No sooner had the winning team photo been snapped, than I was headed back across the field in the direction of the trailers—to poultice the horses and drive them back to their barn or pasture for rest.

Once I began playing professionally, I was willing to sacrifice whatever was required. I missed a best friend's wedding because

---

24   In today's age of specialized concentration on just one sport (I am guilty of parenting this way too, when it comes to my sons' soccer) it is difficult to imagine waiting until age twenty-three to narrow it down to just one. But this is how I did it. Ironically, going to college (and playing lots of other sports) enabled me to reach 10 goals.

the overnight flight would disturb my pre-game regimen; and I routinely shortened or skipped family gatherings, to the point where my parents told me "there are things more important than your next polo game." I wanted to play, and be around, the best polo that would have me. So I chose to forego short-term monetary gains for longer-term improvement, for example, prioritizing a high-level practice over getting paid to play in a low-level game. My rationale for avoiding lower goal commitments was that "the only way to make decent money was to get *really* good." Perhaps my college degree provided the rescue net which allowed me to take these risks for greater improvement—*if I can't make this work, there are plenty of other things I can do.*

In 1988 I got my first opportunity to play with a world-class teammate, Alfonso Pieres. We played tournaments together in Palm Beach, Florida, clicked on the field, and he invited me to keep playing with him for the next season in Greenwich, Connecticut. He was 10 goals, opinionated, and winning everything at the time.[25] Alfonso became my mentor, as well as a source of confidence—"if you think you're right, keep fouling until the referees learn," he told me one time. It might not have been the best advice for winning that next match, but the empowering message I took was to believe in myself. He's a friend I continue to count on for advice.

By this time, I was also serious about one girl. Shelley was still in college for the first two years of my polo career, which meant I didn't have a lot of motivation for going out-on-the-town—and I liked it this way because I didn't want anything to distract me from playing my best. We visited each other on holidays and lived together in New Haven for the first summer I played in Greenwich (while she toiled over her notoriously difficult Organic Chemistry

---

25   Alfonso was winning major tournaments in the US, with White Birch, and in Argentina, with La Espadana, six-time winner of the Argentine Open in Palermo.

assignments). Even before Shelley became a veterinarian and was directly helping me with her advice, training, horse-care and acupuncture needles, I understood our relationship to be a source of stability and an overall benefit to my career.

The last factor linked to my initial success as a professional was horsemanship. I could always ride—at least after I stopped dreaming of Scooter—and the experience of playing many loaned (and often difficult!) horses as a kid gave me the adaptability to get the most out of what I had to play. I studied the horse practices of those with years of experience and was always open to trying new ways of doing things.[26] In 1993 I wrote a magazine article *"What Makes a Good Pony?"* largely to have the opportunity to interview five experts comprising "my list of high-goal horse intelligentsia."[27] And through Shelley, with her holistic approach to veterinary medicine as well as her belief that these animals deserved the best we could give them, I learned to become a good custodian of my horses. *Give them everything, and you can ask everything of them in return,* summed up the philosophy that Shelley instilled in our barn. If there was a question about whether a horse could play with an injury, I deferred to her. If she decided it was worth the risk and could play, I played the horse with confidence. If not, I made the best list I could with ponies available. No second thoughts! I trusted her judgment and she intuitively held the long-term vs. short-term interests of our horses properly prioritized.

---

26 I attended a natural horsemanship clinic with Buck Brannaman at Wildwood Farm in Memphis, Tennessee. I took notes from experienced bitting masters like Hector Barrantes and Tommy Wayman. "Play the horse in what it plays best in," Tommy told me. And I got more confident changing bridles. And Owen Rinehart represented a valuable source of advice from someone who had mounted himself at the top of the sport for many years.

27 I interviewed Owen Rinehart, Carlos Gracida, Cody Forsythe, Alvaro Pieres and Alan Kent in this piece for the jumping and polo periodical, *Sidelines*, December 1993, p. 5.

These essential elements helped me to become a very good player, but I was still far from the perfect 10 goals that every professional dreams about. In January 1997, when I received a phone call from a UVA graduate student requesting an interview for a paper on polo, I was thirty-two years old and had just been lowered from 8 to 7 goals. Even though the horse helps prolong the human athlete's playing career often into their forties, these numbers sounded scarily like the start of a decline.

Stiliani (Ani) Chroni flew in to Palm Beach to interview me along with five other high-goal professional players about our perceptions of competitiveness in the sport of polo.[28] It turned out her "paper" was a dissertation—the final step towards her PhD in sports psychology. During my son's nap, we sat down with a tape recorder at my rented apartment in Palm Beach Polo. She was diminutive, with black hair, olive skin, and glasses that made her look studious; it seemed odd that she was from Greece, since I knew of no polo there. In perfect English, Ani explained that she became acquainted with the sport while working as a teaching assistant at UVA, where several of her students played on the school's intercollegiate polo team. Then she began prompting me with her questions: *What do you like about polo? Why do you play? What does speed and danger make you feel? What attracts you to competition? Are the horses competitive? Can somebody be too competitive? How does competitiveness relate to winning? What does motivation mean to you? Where does happiness come in? What do you mean by talent, ability, and natural ability?*[29]

---

28 Memo Gracida, Owen Rinehart, Mike Azzaro, Julio Arellano, and Hector Galindo.

29 Chroni, Professional Polo Players' Perception of Competitiveness, May 1997, University of Virginia.

Through the course of this exchange, I began evaluating my own responses to these questions. Some answers conflicted with things I'd already said, others sounded hesitant or limiting towards my stated goal of "winning major tournaments on a consistent basis." Concerning when I'm playing my best, I answered: "when I'm being creative and spontaneous on the field." But I lamented that "I sometimes prepare so much that I get mechanical."[30] She also asked, "how good (I) want to be?" and my response, "I try not to get consumed by the handicap thing, but it's difficult because we have this number attached to our names," illuminated my feelings about my handicap having been lowered.

At one point Ani questioned why I would waste time and energy worrying a lot about everyone else on my team, if they were largely out of my control. She prodded, "Is there really anything you can do about anybody else on your team?"[31] It dawned on me that even though I'd played competitive sports my whole life, I had a lot to learn from this person. So I asked her to work with me.

Ani consented to work as my performance consultant, we decided on terms, and she began assigning me homework. *Keep a journal about your feelings and any weird thoughts about the game. Study the back issues of* **Polo Magazine** *and take notes on all the "Instructors Forums"[32] written by players rated 7 goals and above. In your journal, list the strengths and weaknesses of your upcoming opponents the night before the night before the game*—so that I could drop the analytics closer to game time and avoid getting "too

30   Chroni, p. 117 and p. 121.

31   Chroni, p. 122.

32   This is a section of the magazine where a professional will write their pointers and instructions for one specific play. I recall a superb one written by Carlos Gracida, called *Going To Goal*.

mechanical." Completing these assignments required time, which I had, and research and writing, which I enjoyed. It recalled being back in college—where I had chosen to major in history partly because I enjoyed the elements of research, critical thinking, and writing—the only difference being that now everything I learned seemed to reap immediate rewards on the playing field. It felt like a whole new inner world had opened up.

Leading up to my first tournament finals of 1997, I was so excited I couldn't think straight. I had done all of my preparation but the nerves were taking over. Our team was an underdog, I was playing my favorite #3 "quarterback" position, and now we had made it to the finals on Palm Beach Polo's stadium field. Over the phone from Charlottesville, Ani advised me to *remember to breathe*. And, for the entire finals, that became my focus. Riding out on Kanji for the national anthem and opening bowl-in,[33] I told myself to *breathe*. When my mind became distracted by a mistake or a bad call from a referee, I remembered my only real assignment—*to keep the air flowing in and out*. Since it was the only breathing technique I had been exposed to, I focused on the three-part yogic breath that I had practiced some in yoga class—stomach, ribs, and sternum. Ani felt that the 42 minutes of action that comprised a match was a considerable amount of time to remain completely focused. Therefore, for the short 3-minute breaks between chukkers we developed a strategy to help me relax. Whether I felt I needed it or not, I would sit in a chair, glance at my index card with a couple of performance reminders, and take three deliberately slow breaths—before jumping on my horse and heading out there into the frenzy of

---

33   A polo match commences with a throw-in or "bowl-in" at center field. It is similar to a face-off in hockey, but with all eight players involved.

the next chukker. The exercise of consciously breathing through a match was new to me. That finals passed in a blur, I played my best, and the result was the one I preferred.

Thus began a long-term working relationship that changed my career. In the early stages, our work revolved around one basic tenet: *don't worry about things that are out of your control.* Field conditions, umpires, the weather, the draw of a tournament, and the opposition's good horses represented just a few of the things in this category. Many of my habitual worries could be sloughed off altogether, since they were outside my sphere of influence. And, as measure for these concerns, *The Serenity Prayer* provided the perfect template:

> *Grant me the serenity to accept the things I cannot change.*
> *The courage to change the things I can;*
> *And the wisdom to know the difference.*[34]

Ani called me out on my propensity for belittling the accomplishments of higher-rated Argentine players. "Of course they're good, they grew up playing 30-goal polo!" I was wont to say. This rationale had become an excuse for my difficulty in competing with the best players in the world. And she was adamant that this line of thinking wasn't going to get me anywhere. "Baloney!" she exclaimed. "If you could get to 7 or 8 goals without growing up *playing 30-goal polo*, just think how good you are!" This was a new way of thinking . . . and it made me feel a whole lot better. She instilled in me the belief that we are largely in control of our own thoughts about ourselves (one definition of confidence I like

---

34 Reinhold Niebuhr, American theologian and ethicist, 1892–1971.

is: *thinking good thoughts about yourself*[35]). And she encouraged me to watch and ask questions of any world-class players that I could find a way to approach. If I could appreciate their amazing skills—rather than bemoaning them—then I could begin to learn something from these Argentine players.

The pre-game nerves and jitters I described as part of "my love/hate relationship" with being so competitive[36] she understood as not only natural, but shared by most top athletes of all disciplines. And likely, this same jolt of adrenaline was the reason I was attracted to sports in the first place. Rather than becoming disturbed by these butterflies, I began treating them as a welcome sign that I was alert and ready to perform at my very best.

Ani's credo was that, especially in competition, you *do good by doing right*. She saw integrity as an integral component of a healthy level of competitiveness. Consequently, it was absurd for me to revel in the bad luck of an upcoming opponent—that their best pony was temporarily sidelined or that they were playing with a strained jockey muscle—because I thought their misfortune could make the game easier for my team to win. Not only was this line of thinking distasteful and unethical, Ani found it counterproductive to the achievement of my goals. Since I needed my competitors to bring out the best in me, in an ideal world, I should want them performing at their very best (no pins and voodoo dolls). In other words, a world-class opponent playing great is best considered as a partner, each of you pushing the other towards new personal limits.

---

35   Dr. Bob Rotella, *Golf Is a Game of Confidence*, Simon & Schuster, 1996, p. 11.

36   Chroni, p. 116.

This was a novel idea for me. To this point, I had been quite reticent about my routines. After all, I didn't want to give away any trade secrets or competitive advantages! But Ani insisted that the more one gives, the more one is likely to receive. And with practice, I found this to be true. I began asking players I respected to stick and ball with me, or invited them to breakfast to initiate a free exchange of ideas and personal techniques—hopefully to benefit both of us. I offered everything, and I learned a lot! Over eggs at *Gabriels*[37], 10-goal Argentine, Pite Merlos, advised me to "go for 10," because it is "something special you should experience. People look at you differently!" I decided I wanted that experience—but it still seemed a distant dream. For my part, I brought teammates and competitors alike to yoga class and even gave them Ani's phone number when they enquired about doing sports psychology work of their own.[38] As I rose in handicap from 7 to 8 to 9, I was giving them access to the tools that were evidently working for me. In our own way, all of us high-goal players were pursuing excellence. A bit of collaboration proved a very helpful thing.

Billie Jean King said once that "winning isn't that big a deal. The real joy comes from the very thing that involves people in the first place . . . the fun of execution, the fun of playing."[39] I came to realize that my focus on *winning* was not only overrated but possibly even detrimental to my performance. One time I made

---

37 My favorite family-owned breakfast spot in Wellington, Florida.

38 One of my fiercest rivals asked me for Ani's contact info. When we played against each other, it was like war. But I gave it to him. And they did some work. In England one season, another top player (an opponent at the time) asked to chauffeur Ani for her return trip to Heathrow in order to "pick her brain." She was open to the consultation, and the player (and his wife) drove her to the airport. A couple weeks later his team beat ours in the Gold Cup.

39 *Thinking Body, Dancing Mind,* by Chungliang Al Huang and Jerry Lynch, Bantam Books, 1994, p. 205..

the mistake of mentioning to Ani that "I'd rather play badly and win, than play well and lose." Mediterraneans are known for their emotions, and she nearly blew a fuse. If I couldn't be happy with a great personal performance, regardless of the scoreboard, then my sense of contentment was based on things largely out of my control! *Where was the logic in this?* After all, there were four opponents and thirty-odd horses, over which I had zero influence. And we had already established that I effectively could not control even my own teammates. In the end, the only thing firmly in my court was my own performance. I accepted her reasoning and agreed to try to enjoy my strong performances, regardless of the results. So I stopped looking at the scoreboard while I played the game. And sometimes, at the end of a close match, I'd have to glance at my teammates to see whether we had won, lost or tied.[40] I wanted to win more than ever, but now I comprehended that my performance—how my horses and I played—was the only thing I truly influenced. Anything that could distract me from full focus on my performance—speculation about the outcome for example—had to be put away for another time. In other words, I was increasing my chances of winning by not thinking about winning.

I worked hard on detaching from the result-thoughts that could drift uninvited into my head before and during a match. I was better off riding my horses, checking my mallets, or visualizing my set-play assignments than contemplating potential outcomes for an upcoming match. But sometimes I was unable to keep these thoughts at bay. So I'd enjoy them if they were good, block them out if they were bad, and then imagine—as

---

40   Ties in polo are broken by an extra chukker of sudden-death overtime, like a "golden goal" in soccer.

I closed the electric garage door on them before driving to the field—that I was locking them away back at the house. "From here all I can do is play," I liked to remind myself. Sometimes grooms in the barn asked, "are you gonna' win today?" (I hated this question because I was trying not to think about winning or losing. And I was superstitious about simply responding "yes"). I might respond that "I *prefer* to win" or, since often the exchange was in Spanish, "*Ojala*" (if God/Allah is willing). It was my preference. I had all the chances and would take them. But if it didn't happen it wasn't the end of the world.

The author of *Zorba the Greek*, Nikos Kazantzakis, wrote in his own epitaph: *I expect nothing. I hope for nothing. I am free.*[41] This epitomizes the attitude I tried to foster before each match.[42] Very early on in my sports psych tutoring, I went to watch another game in our bracket, the result of which would determine whether my team made it through to the semifinals. It felt like life or death, and it was 100 percent out of my control. "Don't worry about who wins and loses," Ani advised me, "watch how they play the game." And I learned, that this was where my own pre-game focus needed to be directed—how to play the game.

Once that first ball was thrown in, I sought to immerse myself in the action and connect with the play inside the boards. My goal was to play **my** game, to finish plays, to keep the air flowing in and out, and to play creatively with a nonjudgmental mind. Maybe I could even enjoy the experience. *OK, next play* became the verbal on-field performance reminder for keeping my mind in the present. The idea was to say these words aloud to myself after

---

41   *Thinking Body, Dancing Mind,* Huang and Lynch, Bantam, 1994, p. 175.
42   I played approximately sixty to eighty matches per year, for the busiest decade of my career 1997–2007.

every single ball play I made. The *OK* represented a statement of acceptance (no matter whether for a great goal or a bonehead mistake) and the *next play* served to bring my attention back to what mattered most—the play at hand. I said this phrase aloud so often that sometimes I heard opponents (usually those who had previously been teammates) verbalizing my mantra as well. But that was *OK*, too. Maybe it was even part of Ani's plan?

The structure Ani provided, and my complete trust in her strategies[43], brought a whole new level of confidence to my play. No matter what could go wrong on the field, I knew I had the mental tools to turn things around. One reason these techniques proved so effective was that I was prepared to embrace them. My first exposure to mental training had been my junior year at Yale when our hockey coach[44] hired a sports psychologist to work with the squad for a two-week period. I recall lying on the rubber flooring of a locker room in Anchorage, Alaska in skates and full equipment. Through his audible guidance, we imaged some mistakes and bad plays, held them in our mind, and then visualized holding a chalkboard eraser and wiping them clean. Next, we recalled the feelings of executing our best plays and, trying to hold onto this sensation, we charged out onto the ice for the first period of the Christmas tournament. Even though it was only brief exposure with a large group of hockey players, many of whom treated it like hocus-pocus, I liked the sense of calm this session instilled in me. It seemed apparent that positive imagery could only help my play. Unwittingly, I had engaged

---

43   At a Barnes & Noble book signing for renowned golf Sports Psychologist, Dr. Bob Rotella, he inscribed: *Keep on loving the challenge! If Ani says it—trust it!* He had served as one of Ani's professors at UVA, and his words gave me further confidence in what I had already sensed.

44   The late Tim Taylor, an excellent and cerebral coach. He was always an innovator, adapting Russian drills he learned through his Olympic coaching experience.

in a form of visualization when I was a squirt ice hockey player pretending to score goals in the mirror of our foyer, as I waited for my ride to the rink. So, even before I began to play polo professionally, I liked to lie on my bedroom floor (later it was a hotel room or rented apartment) and image myself on the field, playing the way I wanted to. Sometimes I'd go through the chukkers one at a time—and even the horses I'd be playing—scoring goals, hitting good back shots, and executing passes. It helped me establish a sense of confidence that "I can do this" because, at least in my mind's eye, I'd already done it.

Yoga was an additional reason why I was fertile ground for the influence of sports psychology. During the winter of 1996, Shelley began taking yoga classes in Florida. She was always engaged in some form of exercise—dance, riding, running, pilates—and, when pressed, she would even teach exercise classes for other polo wives and girlfriends. I assumed yoga was just one more form of exercise to be added to this list. But it became much more—for both of us.[45] "Adam, if you really want to help your polo, you should start practicing yoga," Shelley informed me one day. That was enough for me . . . and almost immediately I began attending the same Sivananda class that Shelley took.[46] It provided off-horse exercise that I needed anyway, helped balance the one-sidedness of my daily polo routine (reins in the left hand, mallet in the right), and I enjoyed it. I had reached my early thirties, and this practice increased my flexibility and served as key to preventing, or at least minimizing, the effects of injuries. These classes also brought a sense of peace amid the tension of weekly tournament

45 Today, Shelley is a White Lotus certified yoga instructor and teaches workshops as well as three classes per week at Aiken Yoga Studio in Aiken, South Carolina.
46 This class was expertly taught by Anne-Laure Michelis at various venues in Wellington, Florida.

polo. The act of mindfully breathing for sixty to ninety minutes a couple times a week, while performing *asanas* (yoga postures) on my mat has continued to prove an excellent way of keeping my "feet firmly rooted to the ground."[47] So when Ani told me over the phone to *remember to breathe*, before my first finals of the 1997 Florida season, I had just started to work on consciously inhaling and exhaling—at least on my yoga mat.

In my office, milk crates and filing cabinets bulge with my personal polo journals and completed homework assignments. Ever since that first interview, Ani has continued to ask good questions and I do my best in answering them. She laughed at some of the monkeys I described as climbing on my back as I played the game or approached an open-goal penalty shot.[48] And sometimes this response, from across the world in Greece, was the best antidote to my worries.[49] Ani would never take any credit, "I did not do anything," she'd say when I thanked her (usually after a big win), "It was you who prepared and played the game." It might have been *me* who did those things, but it was certainly Ani who kept pointing me in the right direction.

By the time I was raised to 10 goals at age thirty-eight, the support system I possessed was so strong that there were no excuses for not playing well. My wife Shelley travelled with me most seasons and supported me as wife and veterinarian. I teamed with talented players (amateur as well as professional) and, in Bento and Bete, I had consistent, loyal grooms who looked out

---

47   Baron Baptiste, a yoga teacher, used this expression in his video, *Unlocking Athletic Power*.

48   These are undefended free hits from 30 or 40 yards, a bit like a free-throw in basketball.

49   One day I called her all worried before a tournament. "I don't see any way to do well—I'm playing with a bunch of loose cannons!" She found this hilarious and advised me to join them so you can be "four loose cannons running around like crazy." I won't name names, but we won that 18-goal tournament in Boca Raton.

for my interests. I owned a phenomenal group of horses (in fact, recognizing these athletes was a major motivation for writing this book). And I had a mental coach in my corner, whose goal was to make my mind the strongest asset I had on—as well as off—the polo field.

Scrapping for the ball in Outback 40-goal Challenge.

If it was somewhere written in the stars that I would be a 10-goal player, its achievement definitely followed an unorthodox path. But whether karmic or logical, I don't think it could have happened for me any other way. Through going to college, I learned skills—thinking creatively, meshing with high-level teammates, captaining a team, researching and writing a thesis—that proved essential to my ability to grasp opportunities, roll with punches, and *do my homework*. I also met my wife and partner, Shelley. Her influence in the barn kept my horses sound and flying on the polo field; and her monumental efforts at home allowed me to experience the joys of family without major inhibitions on my career. Alvin Ailey called "the idea of freedom through discipline—beautiful."[50] I possessed the discipline but it was only through guidance that I understood the objective of all of this work to be a sense of freedom on the field. *Let go* (of result thoughts) *don't think* (my body knows how) and *just play* (the game). It is never easy, and the practice of mindfulness is never ending, but I continue to find it worthwhile. "They may beat your team on the scoreboard," Ani related, "but they can never beat your mind."

TOP 5 PIECES OF ADVICE FOR THE ASPIRING POLO PLAYER

1. Learn to ride well
2. Don't worry about what's out of your control
3. Watch to learn
4. Find a mentor
5. Play the best polo that will have you

---

50   Library of Congress, www.loc.gov/exhibits/alvin-ailey-american-dance-theater/exhibition-items.html#obj0.

CHAPTER 6

VETERINARY ART & SCIENCE

"The horse, physically and mentally, has natural aptitude for the game of polo, and, if treated well, can have a long, successful career."

This has been my premise for working with polo ponies as their veterinarian and trainer. It reminds me to KISS (keep it simple, stupid) and that going back to basics—whether that consists of nutrition, conditioning, or training—is always the good choice. We can't fight Mother Nature; over thousands of years the horse has evolved to do certain things such as drink water, eat grass, and live in herds. The more we can do to keep their lives as close to an arcadian ideal as possible, the healthier they will be in mind and body. The better we can train ourselves to be intuitive horsewomen/men, based on compassion, knowledge, experience and instinct, the better performance they'll provide on the playing field.

I grew up in the suburbs of San Francisco as a horse-crazy little girl. As soon as I could talk (which was, admittedly, late) I professed to want to be a veterinarian when "I grew up." I played with Breyer model horses, read every horse book I could get my hands on, and begged for riding lessons. I really learned to ride though at my grandparents' ranch in central California: like a Native, bareback and across vast distances over rolling golden oak-studded hills. And afterwards, the cow ponies turned pampered-pets-for-the-day would soak up all the bathing, brushing and attention my sister and I could give them. One summer of Pony Club and a smattering of lessons were all the professional help I received; the rest was absorbed by sheer will.

By the time I graduated from veterinary school in 1997, I was married, had a two year old child, and was the proud owner of my first horse (a former polo pony I converted to the sport of eventing). My parents came to visit us in Aiken soon after Adam and I had bought our farm and built our barn. They very obligingly stayed in the tack room on the foldout sofa, while we were in the barn apartment, and conceded that my passion for horses "hadn't been a phase after all."

Although initially I had been leery of the ethics of the sport of polo in regard to horse welfare, I came to appreciate that there was nothing intrinsic about the sport which made it suspect; maybe just that some archaic practices and attitudes needed to be updated. I became committed to giving our horses the best life possible, with plentiful turnout, socialization, and top medical care and nutrition. Our horses played polo and thrived.

As I developed my own veterinary practice, I naturally drifted towards sports medicine and integrative medicine, and became a certified veterinary acupuncturist. Originally, I thought it might be problematic for my relationship with Adam for me to be his veterinarian, but he insisted it wouldn't and we have never looked back. From the very beginning, he trusted my decisions, and I believe he was grateful to cede control to someone who had his back. To this day, we have never quarreled over veterinary treatment or decisions. Through working with our polo ponies as well as my clients' I became very fond of the type. They are just the coolest of horses! They are self-confident, athletic, and beautiful; if they were in high school, they would be voted Prom Queen (and King).

The second best thing about my profession (the first being that I get to work with horses), is that it never gets old. I am always learning. When Atlanta hosted the 1996 Summer Olympics, a plethora of research commenced to study the effects of heat on the exercising horse. One thing they found was that altering the ratio of foodstuffs enabled horses to work under hot and humid conditions more safely. I was able to use this information and, with a local business, Banks Mill Feed, design a unique, top-quality polo pony feed. I attended sports medicine conferences and became fascinated by the research on conditioning, and instituted evidence-based fitness regimes in our barn. Some initial resistance from the grooms and even Adam was inevitable with these changes, but the proof is in the pudding—when our horses were performing so well that other professionals started asking what we were doing, there were proud smiles all around.

My chosen holistic medicine path additionally provided me a neverending succession of opportunities for learning. Classes in acupuncture, chiropractic, physical therapy, and sports medicine all trained me to be a keen observer—to learn how to see with my eyes and also my hands. My examination became the basic physical exam of veterinary school multiplied by 100. I learned to become aware of the smallest cues in order to figure out the complex and subtle problems that keep a sport horse from performing to the best of their ability. Fine-tuning the equine athlete for competition became my calling.

I started to develop my own philosophy of long-term thinking, which is a natural partner to holistic health. For example, if you have a typical medical problem, let's say an arthritic joint, the short-term medical management would suggest a steroid joint injection. This may well get the horse sufficiently sound to play the next game and maybe the full season, if you are lucky, but it compromises the horse's athletic future. Generally, there are only so many joint injections a horse can handle and it is simply putting a Band-aid on the problem, rather than finding its source. A holistic perspective asks for the reasons why it is this particular joint, and tries to address the causative problem. Is there muscular tension in the limb that is causing asymmetry? Is there a spinal problem with compression of nerves? Is there a farriery (shoeing) issue that can be corrected? Is there a nutritional deficit? Of course, sometimes an injection is necessary, but always only coupled with therapy to fix the primary issue. Mammals are complex biological systems, and the horse is no exception. Looking at cases holistically allowed me to keep the long view of the horse's career and well-being in mind.

And going back to my original premise, I believe that if polo ponies are properly conditioned and fed (and have a good farrier and some turnout!), most equine veterinarians would be put out of a job. Wild horses are known to travel about five miles over the course of a day, and eat nothing but grass, and live in herds. If we can replicate this model, instead of sticking horses in stalls and exercising them alone and in short bursts, their level of performance naturally skyrockets. When well-cared for, their stress levels plummet, they dapple out, they are content. When they develop a strong topline musculature, they are physically endowed to do the work that is asked of them on the polo field—run, turn, and stop. It's not complicated. KISS. And they will play for the longevity of a ten- or fifteen-year career. My work with our horses bore out this theory.

After I received my DVM degree, Adam grew to depend on my expertise. He eventually turned over the management of his barn and horses to me, thus allowing him to concentrate on playing his game. With Bento and Bete's excellent care, our established regimens, and my frequent checks and treatments, we always made sure the horses went to the field prepared to the nth degree. My goal was to have every horse in our barn at top physical condition, completely pain-free, and mentally relaxed. Not an easy thing to do when your patients can't talk! But more often than not, we achieved it. We were a good team.

A morning at the barn for me might start with a request. "Hey, Shelley, can you please take a look at Vienna? She coughed in set this morning." And right away, my brain starts humming. Approach a problem with no preconceptions—make my mind a *tabula rasa* to assess the situation. History, signalment, physical exam—all drilled into me in vet school and so oft-repeated—have never become dull to ponder. Don't forget emotional state: the look in the eye, the attitude, the posture. There is so much to see once you start noticing, and, once you remove yourself from the equation. Lists of possible rule-outs running through my mind as I watch, listen, feel. This is what I love—being in the flow, using my senses. And then the truly fun part comes—deciding what to do. I have so many options with my conventional and alternative medicine training. Acupuncture is the treatment of choice for relieving pain and getting the body to homeostasis, but a well-timed NSAID or antibiotic might just do the trick. Herbal and homeopathic remedies are very effective in some cases. Nutrition comes into play, as well as the environment—why not prescribe food or turnout as our best medicine? Physical therapy, whether it be ice, stretching or specific movement, is vitally important. In this case, after assessing Vienna's condition, I decide to give a homeopathic immune-boosting injection.

I ask about the rest of the horses. Turns out (it is Monday, after all) there are three more for me to evaluate. Musica was a little bit stiff on her ankle after playing. I know her history; she came to us two years ago as a reject, middle-aged polo pony; she was sore all over. She received acupuncture a few days ago and today she gets a glucosamine injection. Vee, who has just started back into work, is carrying his head cocked. As I start to do body work on him, he is very tense, but I must get him to relax if I am to be able to adjust him. I have to have one part of my brain breathing slowly, letting the energy from my strong hands work into his fascia, trigger points, and muscles, while simultaneously keeping up a stiff guard (in the practiced form of my elbow) to keep him from biting me. After the adjustments are completed, I needle an acupoint associated with the neck. My last patient of the morning, here at my barn, is another recheck. Sky had been NQR (not quite right) last week, a little off in the right hind, back sore, and had uncharacteristically bucked when ridden, so I had treated her with acupuncture, chiropractic, and a modified exercise routine. Today I watch her trot straight on the hard concrete of the barn, and in circles on the grass. Sound. I feel her, no reactivity. She is ready to go back to full training.

Going to other barns later that day for my calls, I want to watch the horse in its stall or paddock before its owner halters it. A horse's posture and attitude speak volumes. And how it takes its first few steps as it is led—that is often when any deficit will be most apparent. I listen for footfalls, and watch swing and stance of the limbs and placement of the hooves. And then, I get to put my hands on the horse. I empty my mind of preconceptions and allow the sense of touch to take over me—finding the true "read" is as much an art as it is a science, but having practiced feeling acupoints, trigger points, muscle spasms and asymmetries on thousands of horses, it is an art in which I feel secure.

When the treatment begins, I first make sure the horse is soft in my hands, with its adrenaline systems as quiet as possible, in order to allow the B-endorphins to flow. It is an amazing feeling each and every time, when after the first few minutes of work— whether it be massage, needles, Tui Na[51] or chiropractic—the horse takes a deep breath, lets it out with a sigh, then licks and chews. Horse body language for letting it go and saying "I am fully here with you, I submit to you, and appreciate your touch." As my answer back, I am fully with them (I wear a belted pouch to hold all my needles so I don't need to step outside of their energy field after I begin), I am a gentle master, and I continue the therapy with sure hands.

Often the owner calls or texts later to say what a difference the treatment made. I am happy to have relieved some pain. I am happy when they say "I had the best ride the next day" as I am furthering the bond between horse and rider. When people witness my work, they develop a new sense of their

---

51 Chinese form of soft tissue manipulation.

horse—realizing its responsiveness, further understanding its tensions, and listening to its language. The deepening of this relationship helps both.

With our horses, this bond is very intense and deep. I know every horse intimately—their history of training, successes, and injuries. I know where each horse's favorite spot to be rubbed is, as well as each horse's Achilles heel. I am always able to make decisions with the long-term athletic career and well-being of the horse foremost in my mind. Treated holistically, with natural rhythms of feed and exercise, many of our horses play well into their twenties. We achieve this goal because our horses are healthy, happy, and willing partners.

One of my favorite lines from a veterinary professor, even truer today in the age of Google and PubMed:

"You will miss more by not seeing than by not knowing."

I have made it my business to see. I have vowed to not let that statement become true of my practice of veterinary medicine. To continue my education formally and informally, reading, watching great horsewomen and men, and most of all, letting horses be my teachers.

Being a veterinarian is a labor of love. Recompense is moderate. There are no days off; being constantly on call even for a small practice such as mine can be tiring. But I have found no way to exit—I love the work too much, and the horses simply *get under your skin*. Burying my nose in one's neck and taking a deep whiff, I luxuriate in the smell and lose myself in the present moment. The partnership is a "win-win"—horses bring out the qualities in myself I wish to cultivate. I take care of them, ride them, heal them. It is enough for me.

EVOLUTION OF HORSEMANSHIP

Since the days of cowboys "breaking" horses, the vocabulary and practice of horsemanship has evolved. Natural horsemanship, which encompasses ways of starting as well as working with horses, boasts many famous practitioners ("horse whisperers"), different schools, and many dedicated adherents. The basic premise common to all is to understand a horse's body language and mind to be able to use their social proclivities to your advantage, thereby a more solid and gentle connection can be established.

Equitarian initiatives involving horse care also have benefited the welfare of the horse. By focusing on the natural ways of the horse, and trying to replicate them as much as possible despite being domesticated, they foster emotional and physical well-being. These include guidelines for housing, feed, and grooming.

Shelley is a member of the HSVMA, a veterinary organization advocating for the welfare of all horses.

CHAPTER 7

LESSONS FROM TRAINING HORSES

Watching the frolics of a two-year-old filly with whom you are committed to spending a substantial amount of time over the next thirty days[52]—with the ultimate goal of climbing aboard and navigating safely—you look directly into your soul. How honest are you? How trustworthy? Are you worthy of respect? Are you capable of teaching and molding another individual's behavior? Are you smart enough to know if you are falling short on any of the above and need to back up, reassess, and patiently try again? When dealing with an unpredictable thousand-pound animal, there is a lot riding on the answers to these questions. As on the polo field, it can be a matter of life and death.

There is no doubt in my mind that training young horses has made me a better veterinarian, and a better person. Using

---

52 Often "thirty days" is the period of time allocated to start a young horse under saddle.

a soft voice to get what you want. *Check.* Noticing how your emotions affect others. *Check.* Thinking through problems before acting. *Check.* The principles are universal. And the more time I spent practicing, the more it became part of who I am today. It helped keep me on the path towards an oft-repeated New Year's resolution of *attaining more peace in my life.*

Several years ago I wrote down three principles in explaining my objectives for working with our yearlings to an intern. They read like a manual for kindergarten: *I want the youngsters to respect my space, follow a soft lead, and yield to soft pressure.* In working with horses, some of the above is for safety, as you can't tolerate a horse that treats you like another horse, pushing you around and bumping into you. Horses have to be taught that their dealings with humans are different from their equine interactions. But there is also a strong component of respect embedded in my ideas—a recognition that the relationship is a dance of leading and following.

As Olympic medalist and celebrated eventing trainer, Jim Wofford, said:

> *Above all we need a partner, not a slave. We need horses who are supremely courageous, fiercely independent and phenomenally agile. Teach him that you will trust him with your life. Give him the education he will need, and then* **sit quietly** *while he does the job you have very skillfully and very patiently taught him.*

"Sit quietly." A very hard thing for most humans to do—we like to act first and consider repercussions after. We can't help ourselves! However, we are fortunate with polo to only ask the horse for movements that come naturally to her. Watch a thoroughbred, or polo-bred, foal cavort in her pasture and you will see all the movements that will be required of her on the polo field—run, stop, turn. So the goal is to preserve all that innate movement, slip a rider on her back, and then switch control from the horse brain to the human brain. It sounds simple, but there are lots of ways to go wrong—mostly when the human ego gets involved.

Sometimes the best thing you can do is nothing. Have no expectations. Let each training session **not** be focused on you. Instead, work to remove yourself from the equation, *let the horse lead*. If you pay attention, they will let you know when they are ready for the next step. Less is often more at this stage, and sometimes providence will step in and force a pause at just the right time.

As Adam tells it: ***Bag Lady*** *missed a season at age five because she had cut her tongue badly on a lead rope. I'm pretty sure it helped— missing a time when I could have rushed her because she showed so much promise. Then she went on to play from age six to seventeen in the top of my string. Nothing wrong with waiting a little . . . but it took the rope.*

Looking back at the developmental progress of many of our best horses, they often had some kind of minor injury early on which required time off: Chloe got hung up in a fence and cut her foot open; Pumbaa battled an early bout of EPM (equine protozoal myelitis, a neurological disease); Vee popped a splint (a bone issue). At the time, we thought all was lost but, in fact, these delays may have turned out to be the horses' saving grace. By taking a season—or even a year—off from what we perceived as a crucial training stage, they were given more time to mature and develop before being asked more challenging questions.[53]

---

53 Nowadays, I'd like to think that Adam and I have fostered enough quality in our attention that we don't need "accidents" to help us make good decisions with our young horses!

Polo ponies have to exercise an extraordinary degree of independence. Their rider is really a *player*, often focused exclusively on the ball or the gameplay. In the course of a chukker, a polo pony travels the fine line between responding to their rider's every cue while maintaining their own agency. Especially in the realm of safety the horse bears a lot of responsibility for keeping herself out of trouble and dealing with the multiple variables of seven other horses travelling at top speeds, mallets swinging in all directions, and a ball flying through the air at speeds up to one hundred miles per hour. Unlike other top equine athletes who perform in dressage or jumping—where riders control their mounts' every footstep—the movements of polo ponies are not micromanaged by their pilots. Their relative autonomy, and mastery of the game, gives them a strong sense of purpose, so it almost seems like they are playing the game themselves. All their rider will sometimes give them as a cue is a subtle shift of weight, and the horse scrambles to somehow, miraculously, get themselves there. Adam describes it:

> *To be a good polo player, the riding has to be instinctive, because there is **a lot** going on. That is why, on my best horses, I have the sensation of 'playing with my eyes'— I only need to look and we are going.*

Achieving this balance—this partnership—takes time, patience and skill. Giving a horse a good start will serve it well for the rest of its life—no matter what discipline it may end up in. A typical program of training a polo pony can take years. We will start with foals and yearlings learning barn manners (being haltered, brushed, led, tied) and being exposed to the principles of following and yielding on a long rope in the round pen. Two-year-olds will start under saddle, with plenty of exposure and desensitization to ropes flying all around their bodies. The principles of following a soft lead and yielding to soft pressure are now coming from the rider astride: the rider's hands are leading the horse's head and the rider's seat and legs are pushing its body.

By age three, a polo prospect should move well off the rider's aids of legs, seat, and hands; at this point, feeling is first. The rider's body becomes an instrument of touch to feel the connection with the horse's body, integrating feedback into every decision in order to make harmonious movement together. A three-year-old will also learn to "pony" beside other horses, and be taught to neck rein to the point where they can be "sharpened" or "tuned" up. One of my favorite sayings about a well-performing equine is "that mare can read and write!" This speaks to a horse's ability to look so effortless in all its movements, and be so finely tuned to its rider, that it looks to be performing of its own accord.

A prospect is exposed to "stick and balling," moving around a field while the rider hits a polo ball, when they are deemed ready, usually by age three or four. Solo, at first; then following other horses in games of "keep-away." By age four the ponies then start playing slow "green horse" chukkers and get exposed to traffic, which means other horses coming at them from all angles. This is a very difficult part of the process; some horses never really adapt to it. Eventually, if a horse feels confident enough at age five or six, you start popping them into "white pants" (tournament) games. So it's really not until your prospect is seven years of age that you know what you've got. If all goes well, you hope she will be a trusting partner with the heart and talent to be a game winner.

At any stage through this process—and beyond—a little observation can go a long way. Pat Parelli, a noted horseman, calls it "savvy"—learning how to watch carefully, and respond appropriately. Amy came to us as a playing ten-year-old mare. Adam thought he felt something special in her—which was why he bought her—but after several months he was disappointed in her progress. Then two things happened: first, in one of our sessions with our friend and natural horsemanship trainer, Julie Robins (she had come over to work with our youngsters and help us refine our own skills), Adam impetuously brought Amy out to the corral. "She turns with her body and shoulder but her head stays out on the old direction for a while," he complained. Julie worked her for about five minutes, saw that her problem under saddle was mirrored on the ground, and gave Adam some exercises to work with. In about three rides, with some one-rein stops and an exaggerated leading hand, the problem was permanently solved. This close attention to detail is crucial for working with a high-performance athlete who can't talk!

The second thing that happened was that Adam loaned Amy to a teammate for the next tournament he was hired to play (much to the consternation of Bento, Bete, and me, he often did this, despite the increased risk to the horses and financial cost). But, "anything to win" was his mentality, and his worst horses were often as good as his teammates' best, so he was in a position to help out considerably. Adam remembers:

I brought Amy to California the summer of 2002 as one of my last horses, to get to know her. I played her in the first game, and even though Shelley liked her from outside, I felt like she dragged me a little on the stop. When my teammate Mariano Gonzalez had some injury problems with his own string, I offered him Amy. After his first practice on her, his eyebrows rose up a little and he made some comment like "I think I can get her stopping for you!" He played her one match and she looked pretty good. The second game came around—by now some of his injured horses were recovered—and I asked whether he still wanted to play her. "Well, I think I can keep improving her for you . . . if that's OK?" I could tell he didn't want to get off her! He played her the whole season. In the finals of the Pacific Coast Open Amy played two chukkers for him and wore one of his two numbered BPP (Best Playing Pony) saddle pads. This was the only time I remember gaining confidence in one of my own horses through watching someone else play her. In 2006, she played two chukkers (this time under me!) and won the Hartman Prize for Best Playing Pony of the U.S. Open finals. Mariano is still quick to point out that much of the credit was due to him and his training skills!

Even with careful observation and attention to detail, sometimes our best-laid plans went awry. One mare our kids named Yoda, after the Star Wars character, had all the physical attributes Adam liked. She was brown, 15-2 hands, with a tank frame. When he bought her, he was concerned about an excess of nervous energy—she seemed to worry that the boogey man might *get her!* The mare felt she needed to look out for herself, but—being as she played better than she rode—Adam was confident that through some desensitization work he could improve her both on and off the field.

Thus started our two-week course of basically backing-up and starting over again. I call it "going back to kindergarten." For who knew what the mare had gone through as a foal, and during her time on the racetrack? Adam worked Yoda "at liberty" (free of any restraint and following his aids from the ground) in the round pen. He got her stepping over tarpaulins, and putting up with raincoats and plastic bags being flapped around her ears. He rode her in nothing but a rope halter, even bareback a couple of times. He took her on lots of solo trail rides (so she'd begin to rely on him for support), changed her pasture mates (so she wouldn't get too attached to one horse), and essentially spent the time that usually translated towards a horse feeling more comfortable in her own skin and confident with her consistent rider. Towards the end of week two Adam felt:

Yoda was really starting to trust me. So when Shelley invited me to come on a trail ride with her and her event horse Ciao in the Hitchcock Woods, a 2,000 acre urban park in Aiken, South Carolina designated for equestrians and foot traffic only, I selected Yoda as my mount (one aside—since a trip into The Woods required trailering into town, these are intended to be "fun" rides, where the idea was to enjoy ourselves and not have to worry about riding an unruly youngster spooking at every squirrel). I was confident that Yoda would fit the bill, but I can't deny my desire to get a little training in by exposing her to a new environment. About a half-mile into the woods, the Sand River Trail takes a hard left and carves a narrow path through a sandstone cliff to descend steeply for about thirty feet to the creek bottom below. Well, Yoda took one look at this narrow descent with head-high natural walls on both sides and decided that it was the path to Hell.

In a poof my thorough desensitization and trust-building program seemed to dissolve. Yoda balked at each fresh approach, spinning and bolting away from the maw. I tried various tactics: entering the trail from different angles; waiting patiently as close to the mouth as we could get; following Shelley's horse Ciao down the chute. "Act as if you have all day," and usually the horse will respond appropriately. But, as Shelley waited and waited—with growing impatience—I didn't have "all day." Still with me on board, I even tried backing down (though, with the grade, I doubted the safety of this approach). Then a branch fashioned as a whip also got zero productive response.

Eventually—after thirty-odd minutes of failed entries down this short section of trail—I swallowed my pride, dismounted and led her down the path like a dog. I felt like a dog, too (with his tail between his legs) for having selected Yoda as my "fun" horse for the riding date with my wife, as well as for stubbornly vowing to ride her down the trail.

It can be heartbreaking to expose yourself to the immensity of passion a connection to a horse engenders. One of the low points of my life with horses has to be the night we lost Beach Bum. Here is her story:

*Adam and I bought Beach Bum as a two-year-old in Wyoming in 2000 from Mimi Tate. Mimi had found the gorgeous filly on the track in Billings, Montana, and as luck would have it when we went to see her she had a hitch in one back leg at a trot—which was the only reason we could afford her! I thought I could fix her, and so she travelled to South Carolina. After a few acupuncture sessions she was 100 percent sound and good-to-go. And we now embarked on the process of training her to be a polo pony. She was dark brown, small, and cute as a button; it wasn't long before she'd won a special place in our hearts because of her affectionate personality and athletic talent. She was featured in the **Horse & Rider** film, with me riding her demonstrating some training techniques, and she was in every way living up to our high hopes for her. But one October evening, when she had just come home to Aiken from a very successful first tournament—she had played the fourth chukker in the finals—she suffered a severe colic. I drove her to the University of Georgia veterinary referral center, where the surgeons attempted to save her life, but to no avail; I had to face the two-and-a-half hour drive home with an empty trailer. Between the physical exhaustion of an all-nighter and the emotional exhaustion of losing her, I don't know how*

I made it home. I do remember stopping at Waffle House for a coffee and being vaguely aware that people may have been keeping their distance from an obviously distraught, perhaps crazy, woman . . . . We still miss Beach Bum.

I am convinced that one of the reasons that horses are so beguiling is that they demand—for safety, of necessity—that we pay close attention to them. This is particularly true in a "training" situation. Thus, it fosters a focus of the mind that in and of itself is a state to which humans gravitate. To paraphrase psychologist Mihaly Csikszentmihalyi in his acclaimed book, *Finding Flow*, flow experiences are characterized by high-skill and high-challenge demands, as well as having clear goals and feedback. He argues that the human brain is wired to perform its best under these situations, as well as find serenity. With horses being the intelligent and adaptive creatures they are, every session with them meets these criteria. There is a constant, *live-wire* connection between horse and rider joining the two lives.

A BRIEF HISTORY OF THE HUMAN-HORSE BOND

Horses have lived in close contact with humans for at least five thousand years. They were most likely first used for transportation, and over the centuries have powered human progress. They also transformed warfare and hunting. Horses' social nature made them easily adaptable to life with humans, and stories abound of close ties between equine mounts and their riders. Today, horses are mostly classified not as work species, but rather companions.

CHAPTER 8

LEARNING TO LEAD
FROM BEHIND

Due to the short periods of time—anywhere from one week to two months—for which polo teams are formed, a large part of a high-goal player's success hinges on his ability to quickly get the relationships and dynamics of their team functioning effectively. Until recently, coaches were rare in the sport,[54] so the highest-rated player on the team typically filled multiple roles of captain, coach and player. Thus, for most of the teams I've played on, the strategic decisions as well as the real-time

---

54   Probably, this is the case for two reasons: 1) there were already enough costs and logistics involved with getting to the field, that hiring a team coach was just one more complication (to be avoided if at all possible); and 2) the phenomenon of professional polo, as it exists today, is relatively recent (late 1970s) and so the sophistication involved in the organized teams is still evolving. Indeed, salaried team coaches are becoming more common each year in high-goal polo.

adjustments on the field have fallen to me. I strove to be a good leader, providing a source of confidence to my teammates, while freeing them to fully focus on their assignments and immerse themselves in their own game. I was often responsible for being a reasoned sounding board for ideas, aiding in identifying strategy changes that could be effective for the team, and instilling valuable reminders and technical advice for the amateurs and lower-rated players. Assuming leadership meant taking on all the above tasks, as well as meshing different personalities towards the common objective of winning polo games. Over the years I have developed some strategies for success in this leadership role, with my learning curve tempered by my share of mistakes.

For a new team that hasn't played together before, I liked to hear from everyone in an informal setting—drinking *maté* (the ubiquitous Argentine herbal tea) over lunch, or while on a horse—about what strengths they feel they bring to the table. "I think I'm really good at *X*, and can help our team if I take *such and such* a role." Getting everyone to communicate their strengths doesn't guarantee that they can or will be incorporated into the team's strategy.[55] But regardless, these individuals will feel better—and therefore play better—for articulating these assets, and their captain and teammates will relate to them better through hearing these personal thoughts. The best team feeling is one of a democracy where different strategies and ideas can be proposed freely, often debated, and ultimately determined through the lens and shared objective of winning the next game.

---

55 For example, if two players both think their strength is staying out of the throw-in to hunt the ball, there is probably only one spot for someone to play in this role.

When players experience a sense of self-governance, they often play better and are more content.[56]

I often tried to get to know team members outside of the polo field and in their own milieu. One of these efforts involved a preseason mountain bike ride with a team member some fifteen years my junior. We biked to an undeveloped gravel pit and pedaled over the jumps on the motocross trails etched in the terrain. At one point I followed him across a 2"×10" plank—which spanned a canal—and fell off. The bike and I dropped into the shallow muck about six feet below and my pubis broke the fall on the frame of my bike. The pain was searing, but fortunately short-lived. I survived to play the season but vowed to stay away from any more team-bonding stunts.

I have learned that asking questions is an important component of being a good captain.[57] Many times, my teammates' response to a question such as "what do you feel we can do better next time?" provides ideas I hadn't thought of myself. Earlier in my career, I would just speak at team meetings and delineate my "well-thought-out" plans. I wasn't that interested in what others had to say. When it came to game time, I thought "I could control them by telling them how to play and talking to them constantly on the field."[58] Today, I have come to believe that moderation, listening, and simplicity are the most essential

---

56   This concept comes from the excellent book on taosports, *Thinking Body, Dancing Mind,* by Chungliang Al Huang and Jerry Lynch. It, along with Terry Orlick's, *In Pursuit of Excellence,* are the two books I never leave home (for a polo tournament) without.

57   Working with Ani, as well as playing on teams captained by Memo Gracida, helped me to learn this lesson—that asking good questions is key to being a successful leader. After one loss in a 26-goal tournament, Memo went around the room asking his teammates, "how did you feel about the game yesterday?" for each teammate (three times) . . . before he weighed in with his own opinions.

58   Chroni, *Professional Polo Players,* p. 123.

qualities for productive leadership. A captain needs to read the pulse of the team to see how deeply into planning and tactics to go. In fact, some of the greatest players prefer little to no "chalk-talks" and, as long as they know who's going to whom on the knock-ins and throw-ins, the rest they prefer to let happen instinctively on the field.

> *With good leaders*
> *When their work is done*
> *Their task fulfilled*
> *The people will all say*
> *"we have done it ourselves"*
> *Tao Te Ching*

Since most teams I have played on do not have a salaried coach, I frequently find myself asking a friend who is not in the tournament to "let me know if they see anything." Sometimes a friend or relative will come and sit in the tent, and offer a few pieces of advice at halftime. You can guarantee that if that game is won, he will be invited back! But many times it is just us: the four players, our grooms, and any spouses or significant others we trust to have our best interests at heart. One time, before the finals of the 26-goal Gold Cup in Aiken, I remember taking some advice from Shelley. She had seen all our games, and had all my horses tuned with her acupuncture needles and TLC. It was extremely unusual for her to give me any tactical input, so I trusted that she must really have a point: "To stand any kind of chance (in the finals) you guys better practice stopping Adolfo from going by you so easily in 1v1's!"[59] In our first match-up in

---

59 Adolfo Cambiaso is the best polo player of all time.

league play against Adolfo Cambiaso's team, *New Bridge*, he literally had a field day, passing us like pylons and scoring many breakaway goals. And so, for the afternoon before the finals, my teammates Mariano Gonzalez, Martin Zegers and I took turns pretending we were Cambiaso—zigging and zagging, stopping and starting with the ball—so that the others could practice their *mano a mano* defensive skills. We laughed, and prepared, and argued over which of us had done the best job at impersonating him . . . and the next day it almost worked! We lost in the sudden death overtime chukker after the bad luck of having our goal shot bounce off a horse's foot in the middle of their goalmouth. Adolfo scored the game winner, but it wasn't on a breakaway.

I had to learn to combat my natural inclination to be a control freak, and remind myself to leave everyone in peace—not only teammates, but also grooms, players, coaches, managers, and veterinarians—to perform their own job. I used to find it difficult to "let things happen." On one team in 2001, I was given *carte blanche* to create a winning team. I hired a coach for our team—a respected former 9-goal player—but before our first match of the Gold Cup organized a "secret" team meeting with just the three professionals. My theory was that we would be calmer going onto the field if the three of us just got together in a casual setting. He found out, however, and was furious, and we lost the game. After that, we held traditional team meetings with all the members of our team, including our sponsor and coach, present. It was a classic case of my unproductively overthinking things.

At other times, I have been known to keep my teammates in a state of confusion on the field as they try to keep pace with my rapid-fire tactical changes. Here's a journal entry I made in 2000, after returning from a week-long tournament in Point

Clear, Alabama: *as I waited for sleep to take me and enjoyed getting reacquainted with my thin down pillow, I relived the series of games in my mind's eye . . . and started chuckling. Shelley popped up in bed—worried over this uncharacteristic display of mirth—"what's so funny?" she asked. "Poor Rory and Chris," I explained. "I just realized that, for every single game of the tournament, I would start them in one position (either #1 or #4) only to switch the two of them at some point during each match . . . they never finished a match in the same position they started. We won the tournament, but they must think I'm crazy!"* When it came to polo, Shelley **knew** I was crazy, and she got hysterical upon hearing the story. It is an excellent example of when a coach would have been helpful to calm my on-field tactical jitters, and prevent me from second-guessing my decisions. At one point, Ani developed the strategy that I had to give my carefully prepared game plans not one, not two . . . but three chances to work before I was allowed to make a tactical change.

For a newly formed team I played on in England in 1999, I brought in Ani to help whip us into shape preseason. My teammates thought this was pretty strange stuff. In fact, my sponsor, who had agreed to pay for her visit, rationalized the expense as follows: "well, if it makes Adam feel good, then it's good for the team." And he compared it to his last high-goal professional teammate's desire to have a massage therapist around all the time. There was definitely some stigma attached to having a "mental coach," but at this point, I didn't really care what anyone thought, as long as it helped my team play better. My goal for our first match was to go on the field with zero excuses, having taken care of every possible thing within our control. In our first team session with Ani (one of my teammates had quipped that it was our "group therapy session") we sat in a circle in comfortable chairs in the polo stable's clubhouse. Our first exercise was to go around, by turn answering Ani's question "what we expected or desired through working with (her)." The answers were fairly predictable—"get my nerves under control," "help me not to worry about my horses," or "how not to despair when I miss a goal"—until it got around to my Australian sponsor's turn: "To get laid more often . . . that's why I play polo." Ani (at the time, a twenty-nine-year-old married mom) missed a few beats—while the other three of us cringed—and then jumped back in pretty quickly: "do you feel *playing better* can help you with this goal?" I am not sure if this short burst of sports psychology training had a beneficial effect upon our team; it is a hard thing to foist on others.

I learned after one season in Aiken that—unbeknownst to me at the time—my teammates referred to me as Captain Intensity for my propensity to have detailed team meetings, create horse lists and establish numbered knock-in plays. Rory and Chris certainly would have been justified in calling me Captain Indecision after my Point Clear performance! Today I aspire to be a better captain/coach than at earlier stages of my career; with time and training, I have learned to back off some. My teammate, Julio Arellano, once told me—during our first preseason 22-goal practice on our new team—to "delegate less and play more." And, in relation to being the on-field captain/coach/player, this has been one of my mantras ever since. I endeavor to prepare off the field to the nth degree, but on the field play my very best and take care of my own assignments—and trust my teammates to take care of theirs. Finding the right balance between micromanagement and letting go is my key to being a successful leader.

A captive audience for strategy discussions. Half-time talk with teammates Pat Nesbitt and Mariano Gonzalez of Windsor Capital Team at the Houston Polo Club.

CHAPTER 9

LIVING WITH A
PROFESSIONAL ATHLETE

"Do you mean to tell me that we have spent untold thousands
on a sports psychologist and you can't play a game
without a particular, old, tattered T-shirt?"

I already knew the answer.

Our son had needed red fabric for a school project and riffling through closets in our rental house, I found a balled-up and ripped *Coca-Cola* shirt. It had seen better days, and so I donated it to the cause. I learned later it was a bad decision—it was Adam's lucky shirt. Fortunately, he went on to win that game and my conscience was spared. However, the truth was out: superstition still played an outsized role in his game preparation despite years of meticulous training with a PhD. With his livelihood and,

95

indeed, whole sense of self, dependent on winning, it proved nearly impossible to keep magical thinking at bay.

Game day is when the superstitions make themselves most evident in Adam's behavior. After a "W" in one game, all the little details of how to spend the pre-game hours are repeated: waking up and going for a walk, eating a peanut butter sandwich for lunch, making a carefully calibrated appearance at the barn, taking a nap. These habits weren't in and of themselves bad things to do, but their repetition was nothing but superstition. For after a loss, all bets were off—change it up . . . something, anything. Yes, lucky T-shirts, a lucky belt—he's had them all.

Golfers were some of the first professional athletes to embrace sports psychology. After all, standing still, while hitting a ball that is perfectly still, is the ultimate mind game. Adam was introduced to sports psychology during his college hockey years, but didn't claim it for his own until he met Stiliani Chroni in 1997. While she was interviewing Adam for her dissertation, he had an epiphany: the questions she was asking him could be the key to unlock the door to his success. He seized the opportunity of working with Ani in an attempt to jumpstart his career, which at that time was stagnating. And through this work, he came to redefine his mission: attain a 10-goal handicap and thus reach the pinnacle of the sport. He decided that the only way to continue his career was to be 100 percent committed.

Adam's homework with Ani entailed lots of goal setting. Several times, she had him write out lengthy responses to the question "where do you see yourself in two years, five years, and ten years, both professionally and personally?" Every time he was preparing for a new season, she would ask him to reflect on why he was going. For example, before his 1999 trip to Argentina to play in his first Open, he answered that question as follows:

I am going to Argentina this season to improve my polo. It is a step in the process I have laid out for myself to become a 10-goal player. By playing in this venue with only high-goal players on the field, my reactions will be sharpened, my first-choice instincts will be strengthened as there is no time to second-guess, and my ability to shift focus quickly between the play and the ball will improve. I will learn to pass on the run, rather than checking first then passing. I think it can be a time for me to focus on my own play, and not have to worry so much about the team as I will not be captain. My goal is to play simple, clean polo, and enjoy the experience every minute of playing. I expect to play my best, and I know how! Shoulders back, chin up, smile, and be myself. I will dedicate myself to the process of being the best polo player I can be.

I credit Ani with transforming my husband into a self-assured and confident player and person. In his first years in the sport, playing against better players created the mentality of a petulant toddler ranting against inequities "how can I compete against guys that were playing 30-goal polo in their teens!"[60] Ani, with her usual calm and analytic demeanor, wondered out loud: "Perhaps it means you're pretty darn good if you got to 7-goals without playing **any** 30-goal polo?" That subtle shift in thinking is what came to define the work they did together.

Further developing this mentality, Adam realized he could learn from other great players. He got up the courage to ask current and former 10-goal players for private stick and ball lessons

---

60 A reference to the fact that most of the best players in the world are Argentine, and grow up from a young age playing with high-goal fathers, uncles and brothers.

or if he treat them to a meal to pick their brain about polo and horses. In Aiken, Adam organized meetings at the *New Moon Cafe,* among the highest-rated players in town, in order to "shoot the breeze" about polo and swap secrets and ideas. He became generous with exchanging information. So instead of moaning about lack of opportunities, he cultivated a thought process of "I am fortunate to interact with and play against better players in order to learn from them." A transformation was underway to becoming a mentally disciplined, hard-working adult.

His mental preparation before a game involved many tasks. An index card—containing two "performance cues" and tucked inside his equipment bag to be brought to games—was considered and reconsidered days in advance of a big match. The night before the night before each game, he wrote in his "polo journal," chronicling the strengths and weaknesses of his opponents and then the strengths (only) for his own team. The night before a game he polished his boots. Horse lists were carefully considered (and reconsidered). Adam also maintained a strict schedule for bodily health—following an athlete's plan of proper diet, lots of sleep (and naps), and a regular workout routine that alternated between yoga, running, biking, and personal training. Combining these mental and physical areas of focus gave him a deep source of confidence, allowing him to go on the field knowing he had done everything in his control to play his best.

Polo is nothing like golf, and not only because hitting a bouncing ball while maneuvering a one-thousand-pound animal running at top speed is a far cry from a golf shot. There are simply so many variables—teammates, opponents, upwards of forty horses, field and weather conditions, and umpires all play an outsized role in the outcome of a match. So a lot of Adam's working with Ani involved focusing his mind to prepare *himself* well, and discipline himself to let go of thinking and worrying about all the factors outside of his control. Ani reminded him repeatedly that shedding the excess baggage of the mind—*the monkeys on your back*—was crucial towards being fully present in the game. Ironically—and eventually—Ani's "mental coaching" led Adam towards the goal of *not thinking* while on the polo field. By now, he knew what he was doing out there. The on-field objective was to let his body—and not his mind—lead.

One year Adam exposed his teams to some of his sports psychology reading—in fact, he handed out xeroxed copies—about a training technique of the highly successful Indonesian badminton team. As preparation for international events, their federation had referees purposefully make multiple bad calls in training matches. The players' objective was to remain calm—in spite of the blatant refereeing blunders—and to return their focus to the play at hand. This is a perfect example of keeping your mind in the game and not worrying about what is outside your sphere of influence. During at least two seasons—one in Boca Raton, Florida and one in Saratoga, New York—I heard Adam's teammates shouting the code word "INDONESIA!" whenever a team member got heated over a perceived bad call. In addition to helping keep their minds on what was within their control—namely the next play—it may have had the added benefit of confounding the other team.

In preparation for Adam's 2003 Florida season, the first season he was to play on 10 goals, Ani asked him to answer four questions. How do you want to feel going out on the field? How will you accomplish getting that feeling? What could derail you from getting there? And, finally, if you lose that feeling, how can you regain it? Following is an excerpt from Adam's responses:

I want to feel confident, trusting, and content to be myself. I want to be quiet and determined. I want to maintain my quiet mind. I want to focus in on my favorite polo of the year and remember to enjoy it. I want to feel swept up in the play. I want to be immersed and going for it—with everything—one play at a time.

To get to that feeling I will take care of my body, my mind and my horses. I will steer clear of practicing obsessively and focus more on imagery. I will let monkeys slide off my back. I will look well at the ball, trust my instincts, and score goals. I will be very deliberate and organized about my preparation for each game.

The things that could hinder me getting that feeling are doubts about myself, or about my team, or over-listening to a frustrated teammate.

The way I can get the feeling back on the field is to finish a play, score a nice goal, execute a penalty shot—do something well that is in my control. I will need to find a way to let the game into me and me into the game—maybe breathing, finding my calming "reference tree" (a tree I pick out before the game), looking at my cue words/phrases written on my glove or on the notecard in my mallet bag between chukkers. Off the field, imagery and positive thinking will help me get that feeling back. Knowing I have a great team, great horses, I am at the top of my game, playing the best polo in the world. Smile and enjoy. I know what I'm doing.

He had achieved his goal, and was ready to not just relish the achievement but also to keep working.

As Adam developed more self-awareness, he in some ways became an easier companion. In the early years of his career and before sports psychology training, he was leery of disrupting his "superstitious" rituals, and the chaos and responsibility the family brought was not always welcome. The family eventually became something that was "out of his control," and therefore was tolerated better. And my becoming his trusted vet also changed the equation—the good I did with the horses more than compensated for the distractions.

It is difficult living with a professional athlete. The boys and I would be walking around on eggshells during tournaments, when the atmosphere of the house resonated with his win-loss record. Game days we'd have to vacate the premises for the entire day so he could indulge his pre-game habits. I grew to dread late afternoon games—at least if he played in the morning, the whole day wouldn't have to be spent entertaining two young children at various playgrounds or parks. I got a lot of mileage out of my zoo membership (it was good in Florida, California, and South Carolina)! If I wasn't with him for a season, I could expect regular calls, not to ask how the kids and I were doing, but to ask advice about one or the other of the horses. Although I loved the horses, and always wanted the best for them, emotionally, it was hard for the family to be so obviously second fiddle in his priorities. So although some things got easier, others got harder—for as he became more disciplined about achieving his goals, it was patently clear that he was "all in," and that nothing else really mattered.

To this day, I find index cards in odd places around the house, barn, and various cars with two or three phrases written on them. They are more likely these days to read "enjoy" or "easy" than anything more intense. But those are often just for practice games . . . and I know that the season is really on when I start finding the same shirt repeatedly in the wash.

On Travel and Marriage: His Take and Her Take

Absentee Husband

I often recounted the quote, "absence makes the heart grow fonder," before I embarked alone for another polo season at a distant venue. I said it aloud for both Shelley and me to hear as she drove me to the airport. It represented words of hope. And mostly it has proven true.

Going into marriage we had had some experience at this long-distance love affair, interspersed with charged reunions. Her being two years behind me in college meant that I was already travelling and loving from afar during the first years after my graduation. My love letters from the solitude of the Argentine pampas nurtured me, and, hopefully, Shelley, too. And the fact that we persevered, chose to be loyal to one another—even before a marriage document somehow put more force to this precept—gave us confidence that we were capable of sustaining our relationship in the face of constant travel and separations. I never had much doubt. It was not only that I was "in love" with this person, but I also liked living for some higher ideal. Whether this notion was romantic or real wasn't so important; that ideal had become the person I wished to spend my life (at least when we were together) with. She brought out the best in me.

LEFT-BEHIND WIFE

Initially, I refused to marry a professional polo player because I couldn't imagine a life for myself within that world. I was partially correct.

I had to make myself a place within it that was in my comfort zone (being a veterinarian) and allow him to do all the travelling, playing, and chasing after glory. The inequality of my being supporting staff was one thing that rankled; being left with all the responsibilities for children, home, farm, horses, and my own work was on a wholly different plane of difficulty. I struggled through many days, weeks, and years. But I am stubborn and compassionate, and Adam never gave me a good reason to leave. I loved the horses and the farm and my children most of all, and I reluctantly accepted that none of us were his priority. Eventually, I did demand that some of the travel stop; if I hadn't done that, I don't think we'd be writing this book together right now.

CHAPTER 10

THE UNSUNG HEROES

Driving to my work through the darkness of an early March morning, I am running through the to-do lists of the upcoming day in my mind: trailer loaded by 9:00 a.m. for the practice (and I need to get directions for that field . . . never been there before); oh, and I need to refill the water tank and check that darned left back tire on the trailer, it keeps losing air; and I have the bandages I still have to roll. I hope Cheeca will not be coughing this morning; I'll have to call Dr. Brian if she's not better soon. I pull up to the barn—still dark—and, as I step out and close the car door, I am greeted by a chorus of whinnies. I am eager to get to the light switch and count heads . . . once you have arrived one morning to find one of your beloved charges down and lifeless in the stall, you never quite forget it. Ahh, good, everyone is accounted for, alert and eager to eat breakfast. Heading for the feed room, I remember to add the electrolytes to the grain that is already mixed in the wheelbarrow; it is starting to get hot in South Florida.

And here's the bottle of TMP-SX. Bella needs at least five more days until that wound is healed. As I'm heading down the shed-row, doling out scoops of the individual breakfasts, I think about how well they are doing with the rice bran added to their diet. I'll get them out for a walk before practice, muck out their stalls, then maybe give them each a small flake of hay—I need to order more alfalfa soon . . .

The women and men who are grooms in the sport of polo do much more than just feed and clean horses. They are accomplished riders. They are long-distance truck drivers. They are consummate organizers of feed, tack and equipment. And they are dedicated to their horses as well as their individual player-employer (and his or her teams). Without this wealth and breadth of knowledge—of "skilled labor"—it is hard to imagine that the sport of polo could exist.

People who choose this profession are a varied lot: young and old; male and female; farm-educated and college graduates; any number of nationalities. A love of horses and a love of the polo life cuts across all boundaries. And they come for all different reasons. Some harbor aspirations of playing polo professionally and use grooming as a means of *getting their foot in the door* with

---

3 BEST REASONS TO SPEND A LIFE WORKING WITH HORSES

1. Doing physical labor outside is good for your health
2. Horses don't talk back and are seldom mean-spirited
3. Thinking about horses is the perfect antidote to tech-obsessed 21st Century life

the aim of getting opportunities to play. Others are attracted to the opportunities for travel—a polo groom can see the world. The best do it because they simply love the horses and couldn't imagine a day passing without touching, smelling or riding one—they just couldn't do anything else. Very few do it for the money. And they are rightfully proud of their work.

Are there bad apples? Yes, of course. But these stem more from a lack of knowledge than from bad intent. Polo has been slow to adapt to scientific advances in nutrition and conditioning because many practices are deeply rooted in tradition, and even superstition. There is a huge diversity in the methods used for getting a horse fit to play a chukker and, up until very recently, a lack of any systematic training or guidelines towards this end. And it's no easy task! Polo ponies need to be on an extremely high plane of fitness and health to achieve the physically challenging task of running, stopping and turning for up to 7½ minutes straight. And, because of their sheer numbers (nine or ten horses may go to the field for a single player for any given six-chukker match), the tendency to homogenize a string's exercise (and even feed) is sometimes understandable. So, as with many complicated processes, this one begets many "right" ways. At the end of the day, grooms are responsible for finding their own way, perhaps through trial and error, to get each horse to the field and to perform well. A task that, by and large, they perform admirably.

When Adam and I were in Argentina in 2004, we were constantly getting new horses in the barn for him to try. Our long-time groom Bento had to deal with this rotating cast of characters, and there was one mare I will never forget:

Her name was Pantera, (Panther), and that should have been our clue. You see, unlike cats, horses do not have the paired clavicle bones connecting their shoulders to their sternum; the lack of these joints restricts the movement of their front legs to mostly the forward/backward plane. Anyway, Pantera was extremely wary of humans—likely through learned experience—and Bento quickly assumed all responsibility for her, not allowing anyone else to deal with her and possibly get hurt. Born in the town of Marilia in southwestern Brazil and literally raised on a horse, Bento possessed the horse savvy and steely courage to groom her, tack her, clean her stall, and take her on sets—despite the feral look in her eyes. One day, however, he was cleaning her stall with her standing in the back corner, when some impulse became uncontrollable and she leapt at him, striking with her forefeet. Catlike, she swiped at her prey with her front feet. Bento escaped crawling out on all fours, but only after she had dealt quite a blow to his back. He recovered in a few days; and the mare was returned pronto to her owner. Bento never complained. He just rolled his eyes when recounting the story and affirmed, "Si, ella era una mala!" (Yes, she was a bad one)!

Bento's wife, Bete, can recall an astonishing amount of detail about the hundreds of horses she has taken care of over

Bento and Hale Bopp—what a pair!

Bento and Adam—a long partnership.

Bento, Adam, and Bete celebrate a successful season.

Bete on set.

Bento on set.

the almost twenty years she worked for us. Which leg did Chloe injure in the 2009 US Open final? She knows. What medicine did Duet take when she got the wire cut in Argentina in '04? She knows. What feed were the horses eating in Florida in 1997? She will remember. How to find "out of production" Australian wraps . . . she can do it. And she definitely knows in which specific trunk and location—in the barn, above the workroom, in the trailer—particular blankets, bits, or old fly-masks are stored. She is a master of minutiae. This superb organizational skill is vital to a polo organization simply because the volume of horses, and consequently "stuff" is so immense.

Another conscientious groom and caretaker, Trudy, recently recounted her story:

I am driving through Arizona on the way to the season in Santa Barbara, California. It is June, 102 degrees outside and I have fourteen horses in the trailer behind me, and I'm cursing my boss . . . I wasn't supposed to be doing this alone! The driver didn't show and the horses needed to go, so here I am. Once on the road, it's not all that bad. I have made a life of moving—from New Zealand to Japan, where I caught the polo bug, then on to England where summers are alright, and always the States. Glad to be out of Texas! Can't seem to keep my feet still. But that's ok, the jobs keep coming. I groom high-goal horses for high-goal players, and I can always find work—so travel I will. I feel the horses shift with impatience and hunger. We've been driving for nine straight hours in this oven, following another rig from our team and it's late afternoon before we pull off of I-10 and drive the remaining miles to the Fairgrounds where the horses will layover for the night. Just time left before dark to unload the horses, strip off the shipping wraps I insist on putting on their back legs even with the partitions—can never be too safe!—and let their weary bodies get some sustenance and rest. The pipe corrals look ok. I just need to get the horses hayed and watered. But as we arrive the manager tells us there's a problem: a recent storm has knocked out the electricity to the well and the nearest functioning hose is in a distant building that looks well over two polo fields away. I unload my buckets from the nose of the gooseneck, check my water tank in the trailer and am relieved that I have a few gallons there—enough to give them a sip while I figure my next step. No greater risk for a horse to colic than travelling all day and getting dehydrated. I get the buckets hung, about one-quarter of a bucket of water for each horse. And then the hay, some of 'em won't drink until they've had a munch—only straight alfalfa while on the road. It's not an easy task for me to climb the ladder up the side of the trailer, untie the alfalfa lashed on top, and hurl down two dense sixty to eighty pound bales. When I get the horses hayed, I take the empty buckets from those who have drunk their water, unhook the truck from the trailer and drive the buckets to the distant building for filling. This is a slow process, with water sloshing out the buckets on my return trip. When I am satisfied that the horses' basic needs are taken care of, I go catch some dinner with the boys. But when they decide to go look for their motel, I ask to be dropped back with the horses. I check their waters; I only have fourteen buckets, and I don't want any of them going thirsty. They have another big day tomorrow, even though it should be cooler when we get near the Pacific. I end up sleeping in the backseat of the truck—it's a big soft bench seat, after all, and I'm pretty small. I set my alarm for three hours forward. I'll check water levels, and haul if I need to. Then I'll get a few more winks and be up by 4:00 a.m. to feed and start the next leg of our drive. I settle into the angle of the bench seat and quickly fade out. The horses are dozing on their feet, picking at the remains of their hay, and enjoying the cooler night air as well as the firm ground under their feet. Their well-being is all I live for.

Making the care of animals your life's work means you don't have weekends or regular holidays. It's physically demanding work as well. But grooms enjoy the daily tasks of riding, and watching their horses' dappled coats and sparkling energy reflect the high quality of their care. And being an integral part of a team—not only the player and their mounts but also the larger entity of a polo team—keeps grooms contented over the course of a career. They get paid in dollars, pounds, or pesos . . . and also in the currency of their charges' affection.

CHAPTER II

FINDING HORSES WITH THE RIGHT STUFF

These are the telltale signs: a brooding look; furtive calls; a mind wandering away from the here and now. But it's not an affair that consumes Adam—at least not in the traditional sense—but another pending horse purchase, an obsession with another species of female entirely . . . a mare.

Oh, the search for the perfect horse! Or, if you are particularly blessed, the perfect string—which can mean anywhere from six to twenty ponies, depending on your skill level and resources.

Adam and I have bought all different kinds. Big ones. Ugly ones. Slow ones. And ones seemingly too small. Because the really good ones all have something ineffable—heart. In polo, horses are competitors. They have to outrun, out-turn and out-push the horse beside them. So beyond genetics, beyond training and beyond preparation they have to **want** to win. And Adam's search to find that next one with heart, with a winner's attitude that could help his team win, became an obsession—to the point that, when considering retirement, one of the hardest things for him to imagine was not a life without playing polo, but a life without *searching* for horses.

Adam has taken trains, planes and driven long distances just to go and try one horse which someone told him had some promise. Some of these ventures worked and others did not. But all of them—both the horses tried (and sometimes purchased) as well as the people who showed them—taught him something. Different lessons, to be sure, but always driving home the truism that it is, indeed, the journey that is the fun part. In his words, here are some of his stories.

Wyoming 1992

When you drove into the Tate's Wymont Ranch, you kind of knew you were going to buy a horse. Mimi, a third-generation horse seller, could see us coming! We knew the rules in advance—no swinging a mallet on these polo prospects just off the track (or else the price would go way up!)—and the "trying" basically came down to watching Mimi school them expertly in the dirt arena and then getting a little feel myself, while trying not to feel self-conscious about my ability to get a straight-reining youngster to operate. (Mimi was a tough act to follow.) You were purchasing promise, and Mimi and her father, Bob, helped with this vision by showing photo albums of the Tate horses who had gone on to prominence in high-goal venues in Florida and elsewhere.

On this day, Mimi had a couple of horses "picked out" for me. They were decent and she rode them well. But my eyes kept wandering to a bay filly in a nearby corral. "What about that one over there!?" I finally asked. She was extremely pretty with a low long neck and a big hind-end. "Awww, she's a three-year-old we just got off the track . . . but you don't want to look at her." "Why not?" I asked. "She's too expensive for you," Mimi responded. I was firmly on the hook and it wasn't long before I had purchased that pretty bay mare, Rapid Lady, for five thousand dollars.

Twenty months later my French sponsor, Patrick Stevenson, visited me in Palm Beach to try horses and ends up buying Rapid Lady. I needed the money and wasn't sure if she had all the pieces to be a top mare. I played Rapid Lady in the Deauville 22-goal season that August and she was my best horse. I tried to buy her back, at a substantial profit to Patrick, but he had no desire to sell her. As a nine-year-old she was loaned to Gonzalo Heguy and played all three Argentine Opens (Patrick had wanted to see her play the world's best polo). I was thrilled "my" horse was such a success, but also furious with myself that I had let such a top talent go. Eventually, Patrick agreed to sell her back to me for more than double my sales price, but a positive piroplasmosis blood test prevented her from returning to the States. Rapid Lady stayed in Argentina for breeding and I never got to play her again.

Tennessee 1993

I learned some humility from a mare I tried (and liked) at Wildwood Farm in Memphis, Tennessee. Her owner, Lee Taylor, had faxed a list and description of the seventeen horses I would be riding while on my horse-trying trip. One was described as follows: "Rosey Voyage, Age 9, color gray, dam/sire Super Voyage/Weavers, rider Lee. Comments: played 4 years; bronc; learning to handle, get round, and stay soft; needs more work at speed. Requires detailed instructions to ride & bridle. Be careful. A legend in her own time."

In those days, only a little over a year into trying to mount myself, I wasn't too picky. And—when I learned that this mare could be a loaner—I was willing to overlook a lot. In my trial chukker on Rosey

Voyage, I sat a little deep for a minute or two but then started feeling comfortable on her big, balanced frame. And I didn't feel any humpiness, even though I was aware she had been warmed up exhaustively before I mounted her. When I asked about trying her at my farm in Aiken, Lee reluctantly agreed. He had mixed feelings because he was worried about her bronciness—she had gotten off most of his jockeys at Wildwood, and I knew this—but he would be thrilled if she could go on and perform productively on the polo field.

*A week later Rosey Voyage arrived in a commercial shipper's rig at our farm in Aiken, South Carolina, along with a thick manila envelope of instructions for saddling and bridling. I had a five-hour drive that day to Columbus, Georgia, where I began a tournament the next day. But I figured it would be smart to give her a little spin before I headed off—get her used to her new environment and get me over some nerves about my first solo ride on her. I didn't worry about the packet of mounting instructions. I was in a little bit of a rush to get on the road. Also, I had just played her less than a week before, I remembered most of those instructions anyway, and, besides, she'd be good and tired after that eight-hour trailer ride. So I saddled her up, tightened the girth gradually, lunged her around me in our barn's center courtyard for a minute or so, put a helmet on (just to be on the safe side) and stepped aboard confidently. After I got settled in the saddle, there was a frozen pause and then I squeezed her gently to walk-off—**KABOOM** . . . I had never felt a horse that could buck and spin that hard all at the same time. I had the sensation we were a whirling dervish and I was holding onto the pommel for dear life! After riding three complete revolutions (this wasn't the "spin" I had had in mind!) I finally got off kilter and was whiplashed to the ground quite close to the palenque in the center of our courtyard.*

I picked myself up, loosened her girth, tied her to the palenque and went to go find the thick manila envelope with Lee's mounting instructions. *An hour later, after Rosey had been ponied while saddled on a walk/trot set (with the girth being tightened in incremental stages) I led her out to a nearby pasture—where the ground was a little softer than the barnyard—and tried mounting again. This time I climbed up there (from the mounting-block as the instructions had advised) with a sense of doom. (I was fearful of getting injured and missing the upcoming tournament in Columbus but I knew I had to try again.) Again, she let me get seated, even gently ease my toes into the right stirrup, but when she put her head down between her front knees and started to come undone, I happily obliged—diving for the softest bit of ground I could see. And that was the last time I tried to ride her.*

A week later, Shelley met the Memphis shipper at the pasture where Rosey was turned out with some of our other horses. The man took a good look at the big grey mare and drawled "Yup, thought so! This isn't the first time I've had to pick this one back up."

Wyoming 1996

One of my most reliable sources of affordable prospects was Sheridan, Wyoming and, more specifically, the polo trainers who rode on the ranches surrounding the Big Horn Equestrian Facility. I tried as many horses as I could during my brief, frenetic visits; and it was always a thrill to drive into the club and see up to a dozen trailers parked around the fields with horses for me to try. As I rode one after another, all my senses were alive trying to feel for that next champion . . . or to find the perfect match to fill that order for a sponsor. If playing polo is sometimes described as an addictive drug, trying (and buying) was a narcotic equally powerful.

On one trip, I flew into Denver and rented a car for the six hour drive north to where horses would be waiting for me. It was late spring, still a little early for the Big Horn horse season, but this was the only window for me to get out there before my next tournament season began; my yearly appearances were crucial to maintaining the privilege of first option on many of these green horses. And, in those days, I was determined not to miss a single horse! I overnighted at a motel on the side of I-25 somewhere near Cheyenne. As I started out the next morning at the crack of dawn, eager to finish the drive and to start riding horses, there were swirls of something in my headlights, some dusty substance . . . and it took me a while to realize it was snow.

Thirty miles south of Big Horn, I stopped at a ranch near Buffalo to sit on a group of prospects on my way to the Equestrian Center. I figured I'd save them the trailer trip. It was still early, and the snow had stopped, but there was frost on the ground and our breath was visible as the owners led out a wide-eyed brown gelding called Chaos. His name should have told me all I needed to know. But, excited to start the trial process, I gamely stuck my toe in the stirrup (I usually place the ball of my foot on the stirrup, which means the toe of my boot is sticking an inch or so out the inside of the stirrup towards the horse's belly) and swung up—without a whole lot of thought or preparation—the way I had for thousands and thousands of mounts. I don't think my seat even touched the saddle before Chaos had all four feet off the ground, gave a ferocious buck and launched me into orbit. I eventually landed with a thud, flat on my back on the frozen ground. The horse's owner was quick with his advice: "you gotta learn to keep your toes in when you get on!"

Later that day at the Big Horn fields—embarrassed but more or less unscathed from my incident with Chaos—another cowboy and polo-trainer, Mike Morton, gave me the best description and advice I had heard about mounting—a subject which had taken on a new level of importance for me as I worked my way through the thirty-odd horses I had to mount and try in the brisk mountain air. "You wanna ease on up there like a slow drink of ice water," he advised. I've been doing it that way ever since!

London 1999

When I boarded a train in Euston Station, London, bound for Cheshire—several hundred miles northwest in the English country-side—I could have guessed I wasn't about to find a top polo prospect. It was probably one of my craziest trips—heading off into the hinterland on my British teammate's second-hand referral that someone might have a good pony up there. I forgot to ask how many top ponies had ever come from Cheshire. I had heard of the Cheshire Cat but nothing of the region's equestrian credentials.

Probably indicative of the quality of the mare I was shown is the fact that I have no recollection of her. However, nothing ven-tured, nothing gained, and what I did gain was a nice pub dinner and some sports psychology from my host and the trial horse's owner, Derek Lion, who was the former Captain of the Oxford Rugby team. "I would never criticize a teammate during a game, even if he made a mistake," Derek told me. "I hold the team feeling as more important than correcting that individual who will take it as a put-down. Only later, after the game, can I discuss it with that individual."

His advice was well received and, even now, I try to heed it in my role as the captain of the polo teams I play on.

In the end, we lived and learned, and most of the leg-work did pay off. At one point in Adam's career it seemed like fate had conspired to grant us ownership of what was arguably the best string of polo ponies in the world at that time. But there was also a feeling perhaps that we had earned this because we were good stewards of our horses. Trainers wanted us to have their horses not only because it was good business for their horses to shine on a bigger stage, but also because if they cared about their horses, which most of them did, they would sleep well at night knowing their four-legged trainees were going to a good home. We treated our horses not just as well-oiled machines, but as sentient beings, with hearts and minds that demanded attention too. They more than paid it back to us with their performances on the field.

CHAPTER 12

DREAM TEAM

Adam searched so hard for the perfect string of horses that sometimes he didn't realize he was already playing it. "There must be another one out there . . . somewhere," was more his mind-set. Recently we came across an index card dated 2006, listing Adam's horses for one game of his 26-goal season with the team Las Monjitas, the same year they went on to win the U.S. Open. Any one of those outstanding polo ponies could have been someone's individual favorite. And he had eight of them! It took luck and Adam's compulsive personality—as well as some of the comical and costly trials mentioned previously—to assemble this group. Each with their own story of discovery, these ponies came in all shapes and sizes, cost widely varying amounts, and manifested the type of horsepower, which, in Adam's words "were the main reason for any success I ever enjoyed in the sport." As Alfonso Pieres wisely advised him early on in his career, "it is hard to play badly on a good horse." So at age forty-two, in one qualifying match of the 2006 U.S. Open, here is Adam's horse list, chukker by chukker, with two spares:

Chukker 1: Hale Bopp During her later years, I often started on her in the first chukker because of my predilection for smaller, handy horses. She gave me confidence, all the options, and got me to the ball first. And, even if she might have lost a touch

Going to goal on Hale Bopp . . . no horse had more grit.

of her top-end speed, this was a great way to start the game (in her prime, I had played her in the 4th, as after half-time I again liked to reintroduce myself to the game on my favorite type of horse). She got me goals and won me fouls, and also the opponents were a little scared of her quickness so I gained even more space when I had the ball. She came to me out of the blue one winter when her owner, Roger Redman, called me while on his way to Wellington with a trailer-load of horses for sale. I met him that afternoon to ride the group, but he thought the "little black mare," 15 hands with some thick shoes on, would "maybe suit a woman patron." A couple other high-goal players had looked at her (I won't mention names!) and thought she was too small. I rode her anyway, and instantly loved her—for her breadth, turn and mouth—and bought her the next morning after playing her in a relaxed practice. The same week she played (and was crucial to winning) a 26-goal match—the quickest I had entered a new horse into my best string. And she never looked back! She won six Best Playing Pony awards, including BPP of the Gold Cup in 2001.[61] I remember Shelley playing Hale Bopp in her first practice (in a snaffle!) that 2001 season. She was full-of-beans but following the ball like a cat. "It feels like I'm riding dynamite!" Shelley commented. Hale Bopp has certainly been my favorite for the fun factor. I always looked forward to playing her.

---

61   Best Playing Pony (BPP) awards are given for the best playing pony in the finals of all major United States Polo Association (USPA) tournaments. They are extremely hard to come by, and therefore often deemed a player's proudest accomplishment—even more so than an MVP award. To win one, your team must first make it to the finals of the tournament. If it's an eight- or twelve-team tournament, your odds are narrow. Then, in the finals, each player is bringing eight-ten horses to the field; so, in order to win BPP, a horse must be judged the best pony on the field that day out of approximately sixty other horses.

Chukker 2: Chloe She is really as good as any other horse on this list. The previous summer in Santa Barbara (2005) she had won the BPP award for the finals of the 20-goal Robert Skene tournament. I often choose power-and-handle for the second chukker, and she had it all. She's a little higher naturally with her head and neck—maybe that's why she didn't get as much fame as some of the others—but she stops to zero. And she is very fast (won two to three races on a track in Michigan) and her turn is exceptional to both sides particularly out of the throw-ins, where she maneuvers like a cat. She would go on to play two chukkers in the finals that year (2006). I found her in Sarasota, Florida when I drove across the state to try horses in between matches in Wellington. Like Hale Bopp, Chloe was also owned and trained by Roger Redman. I liked her feel. Roger agreed to bring Chloe over to my barn in Wellington one week

Chloe with Bento before Robert Skene BPP trophy presentation, Santa Barbara, California.

later for me to try again in a good practice and I bought her in a package with her partner, Kate (a huge gray mare that went on to win BPP in one of the 40-goal exhibition matches[62] I got to play in during the years I was rated 10). Chloe played her first U.S. Open in 2002 at age six; and is the only horse that played for me in all three of my Florida-based U.S. Open Finals ('02, '06 and '09).

Chukker 3: Rio Of all the horses I play on this list, Rio has given me the ball the biggest. By that I mean literally that the ball looks big on her because she is so easy to hit off. She is a platform! Rio played her first tournament game at age three; she was as natural as they come. When PBS approached me in 2001 about filming a Nature Series documentary, later to become **Horse & Rider,** we chose her as my partner.[63] They filmed Shelley administering acupuncture needles the day before her first high-goal match, and Bento and Bete taking her out on her early morning exercise set. They used a live match cam on my helmet to experience the chukker as a horse sees it. She was set up for stardom from an early age! She was always easy with an exceptional mouth,[64] and if I had any worry it was that she would to be too slow. But when she played the 2004 Argentine Open, she seemed to find another gear. Plus, I always played well on her because she allowed me to slow down with the ball and find a pass or a shot on goal. As Shelley always reminds me,

---

62   The Player's Support Group is a fund-raising program founded by Canadian player, David Offen, which organizes annual 40-goal (four 10-goal players on each side) matches in Florida. These matches are not only a display of world-class talent—even while players are somewhat relaxed because of the exhibition nature of the event—but also provide a venue for raising funds to help players and grooms in the polo community who may have been injured in the sport. Kate won BPP in the 2003 Player's Support Group 40-goal match in Boca Raton, Florida.

63   http://video.pbs.org/video/1215194821

64   A horse's "mouth" refers to the quality of their connection via the bit to the rider's hands.

Easygoing Rio. She made the ball look big.

your "best horse" is not necessarily the best horse in your barn but rather the one on which you play best. Rio always allowed me to do that. I remember when a polo-playing friend came down to visit us in Argentina and I let her stick and ball Rio, she afterwards exclaimed, "Now I know why you guys get to 10-goal ratings!"

Chukker 4: Duet The fastest horse I have ever played—she flew! As of this writing I'm wondering why I put her in the fourth (when I just explained that I like easy, handy horses in the first and fourth chukkers). Likely, I was complementing my teammates, who probably played their handy ponies in this chukker. Charlie Armstrong, the owner and breeder of many top ponies, called me and with zero pleasantries announced, "I have one for you." She was a Speed Appeal-Elliptical mare that had won several races on Florida racetracks. I was wary when he described her as "having a lot of power," for that is often polo short-hand for out of control! But Charlie was insistent and shipped her up to Aiken for me to try in a 16-goal tournament. She was wide and travelled low the way I liked, and I found her just easy enough (when they run with that much commitment, it's almost impossible for them to stop on a dime). I knew I was playing in the Argentine Open that coming fall[65], and I bought her. She ran so fast that she made the ball look small but—as long as I could hit it—there was no other horse on the field she couldn't run by (or through). She won a BPP in California and played the 2004 Argentine Open season. In 2007, she helped me win the Gold Cup with Catamount, and was my best horse in the finals (even though she did not win BPP). If it weren't for a wire cut she suffered in a corral in Argentina and a clubfoot that periodically gave her issues, I'm sure she would have won more prizes. Significantly she is the only chestnut on this list, as I have a predilection for bays, browns and grays. She, however, was not a typical flighty chestnut; her personality was docile and sweet.

---

65   Because the Argentine Open is unlimited by handicap, the style of polo tends to be fast and running, which suited Duet's strengths.

Duet taking the boards in stride.

Chukker 5: Pumbaa Like Chloe, she has both power and a stop, and her endurance was remarkable. It feels like you're on another class of animal when you're on her; other horses just seem to melt away. When Pumbaa's previous owner asked me at the end of a Florida season to take one of his young mares because he "liked the way (I) rode," I initially didn't want to accept.

I had enough of my own to train and, besides, he was asking a lot of money for her should I decide to buy her. However, after riding her once and feeling her athleticism, I reconsidered, and asked for him to give me a discounted price in return for my work with her. He agreed, and I took her with me to Aiken, and introduced her to polo by playing her that spring in some pro/

Controlling the play on Pumbaa.

ams. The following fall—she was still five years old—I put her in a 16-goal tournament. The first knock-in I took, I realized that nobody on the field could get near me. I knew right there and then I had to buy her, which I did. She won the Hartman Trophy for BPP of the U.S. Open Finals in 2002, and that was after a bout with EPM[66] as well as a tendon lesion (both of which Shelley treated). In her top form, I still consider her the most exceptional pony I have ever played.

Chukker 6: Amy If Pumbaa was the most exceptional, and Hale Bopp my favorite, then Amy was the most "complete." By this I mean she had everything: she could run, stop, bump and turn, **and** she gave me the ball nearly as big as Rio! I can't imagine a better mare than this to play in the 6th chukker! At the time of this game, she was my best. I was so fortunate that in the spring of 2002 in Aiken Amy's owner phoned and asked me to try her horse. The mare—a bleached bay with a star and snip—was already ten years old (which was a bit of a concern) and I played her in a 3v3 practice on the choppy field below my house. Amy had been bought off the track in Kansas and trained by the same person since age two. In that first practice with me, her head darted down low when she ran (which I liked), and she had power, but she felt pretty long in her body and hard to collect. Then I played her in a 16-goal match[67] and I was worried that she might not stop quickly enough; but Shelley liked the way she moved. The price was reasonable, and I took the chance. That summer I loaned her to a lucky teammate in California.

---

66   Equine Protozoal Myelitis is a neurological disease of horses caused by a protozoa and transmitted by the feces of opossums. It can be fatal if left untreated.

67   There is more risk of injury when a horse plays in a competitive match, so it is not often that I could "try" horses that I was considering buying in a game situation. Usually sellers only let one ride, stick and ball, and practice the horses they are showing.

Amy leading the pack amid 70 goals worth of players in Outback 40-goal Challenge.

And when he asked to play her two chukkers in the finals of the Pacific Coast Open, I knew she must be good. In 2006, the year of this list, she played the second and sixth chukkers in the finals of the U.S. Open and won the Hartman Prize for BPP of the day. She also won BPP in the USPA 20-goal Silver Cup in 2009.

First spare: Bag Lady She could run, and stop, and turn to the right like a top. And she's beautiful—featured in my favorite Banks Mill Feed advertisement with her brown dappled coat gleaming as we go through the goalposts with the ball! In the finals of the 2002 U.S. Open, I played her one-and-a-half chukkers and scored a key, tying goal at the end of the fifth. Sadly, she never won a BPP prize. In the fourth chukker of the 2004 Pacific Coast Open finals, I scored four goals on her from the field and she turned the game around. But even though everyone

Going through the posts on Bag Lady in the Pacific Coast Open finals. She was robbed of a BPP prize.

agreed she was the best horse that day, I had robbed her of the prize by putting my two BPP pads on Pumbaa and Hale Bopp.[68] I bought Bag Lady as a three-year-old prospect when her owner

---

68   In those times, we were given two numbered saddle pads to enter for the BPP prize in the finals. This way judges only had to watch 16 horses to choose the best. Anything that did not have a numbered saddle pad (like Bag Lady on this day) was not eligible, even if they were the best horse on the field. Today, there are no numbered pads and judges must select the best horse on the field from all of the horses that are playing that day. I am sure Bag Lady would have won that day, if we didn't have numbers; but I also can't blame myself for wanting to put my numbers on Hale Bopp and Pumbaa.

got out of polo. Mark Bryan (a trainer who later worked with us) was riding her at the time and advised me, "Don't even think about it, just buy her as quick as you can!" He was right. She got the name because she was such a slob with her grain that she had to be fed with a feedbag hanging over her head. With time she learned better manners and, one summer in California, she starting eating Cheerios out of Bete's hand. At age six she played her first Florida season and my 22-goal team's manager[69] dubbed her "the best mare in Florida." She helped me win many, many tournaments including both the '02 and '06 US Open Finals, and was among the best of my string for her twelve-year playing career. I have to thank Shelley for keeping her sound; Bag Lady had a nagging splint[70] from her days on the racetrack, which Shelley treated regularly with various therapies including ice, electro-stim acupuncture, magnets and Sarapin.

Second Spare: Gala She was brought to my barn for a trial early in my 2004 season in Argentina. It took one practice to know that she was my type: balanced, low and wide. Shelley loved the way her broad chest and unique shoulder motion enabled her incredible lateral mobility at speed. Later, with a bridle change from a gag into a pelham, she even added a complete stop to her repertoire. Shelley and I conferred about a diagnosed navicular bone issue[71] as well as the requirement that she would return to her owner for breeding purposes after her playing career was

---

69 Chris Strateman of Orchard Hill Polo Team.

70 An irritation of the splint bone (metacarpal II) and the interosseus ligament.

71 The navicular bone is located in the horse's foot, and any compromise to this bone seen on radiographs present the potential for future foot pain. Gala had failed the prepurchase exam for another high-goal player, and her owner was totally forthcoming with all the information and previous radiographs. Shelley and I decided it was a risk we were willing to take and, hopefully, something we could manage given how well the mare played. These were the calculated decisions we were often faced with, operating on a limited budget.

over. We decided she was too good to pass up. I only got to play her for two-and-a-half seasons, before an unrelated knee injury ended her playing career. She got tired if I started a chukker on her (and I think I may have been worried about her foot), so I used her as a spare, jumping on her for a couple of minutes two or three times a game. She played well in every match of

Gala in the finals of the 2006 US Open.

Hurlingham and Palermo Opens in Argentina in 2004, and then helped me win the 2006 U.S. Open Finals (she and Bag Lady stayed out as spares on either end of the field for the entire game and I got on each of them three times).[72]

There are many other exceptional horses that I was privileged to play. Mirage, Muffin, Baby Doll, Jill, Kanji, Tequila, Cambicha, Spy, Tula and Josephine—who themselves combined for an additional ten BPP blankets. But the list that day had to be one of my best; even now, I still feel a particular kinship with this group. We rose through the ranks together, and achieved some amazing successes. Today, some of their sons and daughters live on our farm and are in various stages of training and playing. It is emblematic of the sport of polo to have a dream team comprised of horses—they are your legs, your heart, and the personalities that make the sport tick.

---

72   Spare horses are the ones that I change on the fly onto typically after four or five minutes of the chukker. They are held in the end zone by "spare holders" at either end of the field so as not to create danger for the spectators on the sidelines. My objective in jumping on a spare is twofold: 1) to minimize the risk of injury in playing a tired horse into the ground; and 2) to gain a competitive advantage by always being on fresh horse. A horse like Gala could play six minutes in three, two-minute spurts (as a spare) and be amazing; but if I had started a chukker on her, she would be exhausted—and we would be losing plays—after three to four minutes. Recently, high-goal players are changing more and more frequently and it is not uncommon to see a player play three horses in any given chukker.

VETERINARY DIRECTIVES FROM SHELLEY
FOR THE LAST 4 WEEKS OF THE CA SEASON
(SHE HAD TO LEAVE TO GET BOYS BACK IN SCHOOL)

Pumbaa: alternate Legend and Adequan weekly; ice old tendon 2x week; EqStim 4 ml IV every Tuesday (in fridge); Cimetidine 2 tablets twice daily

Hale Bopp: keep weight down; check mouth and teeth once a week; ice splint 2x week; give Legend if sore (old stifle injury)

Chloe: if mood turns sour start U-Gard; if sore use 2 ml Traumeel under tongue

Kate: Adequan every 2 weeks; "paint" hocks with DMSO mixture day before games; keep weight down; EqStim 4 ml IV every Tuesday; Cimetidine 2 tablets twice daily

Rio: easy!

Bag Lady: weekly Legend; ice 2x week; Biotin daily in feed; poultice RF foot if sore

Josephine: alternate Legend and Adequan weekly; ice 2x week both front legs; Biotin daily in feed

Amy: alternate Legend and Adequan weekly; ice 3x week both front legs; keep fronts wrapped, sweat 2x week and poultice after games

Muneca: U-Gard daily

CHAPTER 13

POLO ARGENTINO

Rarely does it happen that one country embodies the life and soul of a sport as much as Argentina does with polo. It dominates the world in many measurable demographics: most polo players, best polo players, highest concentration of polo fields and tournaments, largest breeder of polo ponies, and most polo pony sales. This makes travelling to Argentina and learning "barn" Spanish a necessity for any aspiring player. My experiences in the southern hemisphere, complete with stolen luggage and passports, were undoubtedly one of the biggest influences on my career.

As a young player, I had met several Argentine professionals who had played the East Coast Open tournament at Myopia. One of these, Juan Martin Zavaleta, offered me a place to stay if I ever wanted to go down. And so the September after graduation from college I boarded a plane at Boston's Logan

Airport carrying a newly purchased case of Spanish language tapes, $600 in traveler's checks (my summer's earnings), and a bag of polo gear. The next morning as the plane descended towards Aeropuerto Eizeza outside of Buenos Aires, I scanned the countryside for polo fields. I presumed they would be dotting the countryside, but I wasn't sure I could make out any. I stayed for two weeks with Juan Martin and his family at their new farm in General Rodriguez. They treated me like family, but without a car and with very little to do, I couldn't help feeling like a third wheel. I studied Spanish (making exhaustive *que quiere decir . . .* queries of the maid), wrote in my journal, accompanied Juan Martin to his games and practices, and stick and balled one to three horses every afternoon. So when Juan Martin helped procure a work-to-play position[73] for me at the estancia of renowned polo player, breeder and horse trainer Hector "Gordo" Barrantes, I jumped at the opportunity. That same night I was bundled on a *collectivo* headed for *Trenque Lauquen* and an estancia named *El Pucara*.

At 5:00 a.m. the next morning I stumbled off the bus and onto the hard-packed dirt of the tiny village of Tres Lomas. The sun wasn't up yet, and I was glad to find a red Ford pickup waiting with its headlights on in the predawn darkness. I understood very little of the driver's Spanish as he jabbered away on our bouncy trip through wide-open grassland dotted with potholes of water from recent rains. Waterfowl abounded, and we even passed a flock of pink flamingos standing statue-like on their single legs in the shallows of a flooded pasture. Arriving at estancia *El Pucara,* I dropped my gear at the bunkhouse, donned rubber

---

73 This was essentially an apprenticing position, where my living expenses would be covered in exchange for my riding Hector's horses and also learning from him.

boots, and headed to the corrals for my first assignment. From my journal, I found a reference to this first meeting with Hector Barrantes, September 24, 1987: *on my arrival, Hector indicated a couple of dirt corrals with his huge boxer hands and gave me my marching orders: "There are your eight horses. Ride them every day and always have a reason for what you are doing."*

And that is what I did . . . all day, every day. Some evenings Hector and his wife Susie (Ferguson) Barrantes came down to share an *asado* (cookout) at the bunkhouse, where six of us workers/riders lived.[74] The fire embers—and the sizzling meat—held us in a ring as Hector shared his horse history. Replacing the maté gourd he coveted during daylight hours[75] with a plastic cup of red wine, the stories flowed. He talked of a special horse he had bred named Luna, who we would soon witness playing in the Argentine Open.[76] He recounted his involvement with large-scale polo pony sales—literally boatloads—to England. And he reminisced about the feeling of playing back on Palermo's stadium field, *cancha de la Victoria* (field of victory), in the Argentine Open.[77] We were in the presence of a legend, and we knew it.

---

74 We were two Brits, one Australian, one American, and two skilled Argentine groom/players each with a similar allotment of six to nine horses to ride and train each day.

75 Drinking yerba mate is a ritualistic Argentine work-break akin to "taking tea." People typically sit in a circle—and chat—as the *mateador* (mate maker) serves the single-portion caffeinated drink of hot water briefly steeped in mate leaves around the circle. After slurping down their portion with a communal straw, the recipient returns the dry gourd to the server. And this continues in a clockwise direction (with the herb periodically being replenished or the water reheated) until every member of the circle has said "*gracias.*"

76 Luna went on to win the Lady Townley Cup for BPP of the Argentine Open in 1989 and 1990, ridden by Gonzalo Pieres. She is a critical foundation mare to Ellerstina's breeding operation today.

77 Palermo refers to the neighborhood in Buenos Aires where the polo stadium, which hosts the Argentine Open matches, is located. Hector played for *Nueva Escocia* in the late 1970s.

El Catedral, Palermo #1 field.

I worked for three months at *El Pucara*. I absorbed polo knowledge, learned horsemanship skills, and made excellent contacts. I had unwittingly stumbled upon one of the premier polo operations of its kind. Unfortunately, Hector and Susie have both passed on, but the legacies of their horses continue to be among the finest polo ponies in the world. With this experience began my obsession with the country. I returned again and again to apprentice, to buy horses, to play tournaments. I spared no effort to get myself on a plane bound for Argentina. One spring in Hong Kong, in the days before e-mail, Shelley joked that I had the fax machine in our apartment humming for weeks— proposing teams and trying anything to invent a job—before something finally came through. It was a somewhat sketchy deal to play in the *Mundialito*,[78] but at least it meant I could go to Argentina and "prepare for my summer season in England." But

---

78   Paying expenses and a minimal salary unless our team proceeded to the semis or finals. This tournament—"little world"—stipulated two foreign and two Argentine players per team.

upon my arrival in Buenos Aires, it rained for ten straight days, and the tournament was canceled. All my efforts had been for a single practice game that I played. But even this didn't dampen my enthusiasm for the place. It was as if I believed I could learn through osmosis—that simply by being there, in the heartland of the sport, I was improving my polo.

To pay for these trips and "get mounted" while in Argentina required ingenuity. Mostly this involved hustling deals to purchase horses for others—either the team of my current sponsor in the States, or any player willing to trust my ability to find them a good horse. I was providing the service of finding good horses for a reasonable price through my contacts and travel. This was my ticket to getting to play lots of polo. While the very *best* ponies come from all over the globe,[79] Argentina is the undisputed leader in terms of numbers of playable polo ponies for sale. So there was always lots of polo to be played while trying the horses in order to fill these orders.

My home base was usually in the town of Pilar, forty-five minutes drive north of Buenos Aires, at the barn of my mentor Alfonso Pieres. For several years, I played a string of Alfonso's horses in tournaments such as the *Mundialito*, The Patron's Gold Cup and the *Cámara Diputados*.[80] And Alfonso had excellent horses. It was an unspoken arrangement but, in return for getting

---

79   In 2013 and 2014, the Lady Susan Townley trophies for BPP of Argentine Open were won by American-bred horses (Chocolate in 2013 and Lucky in 2014). The 2014 U.S. Open Hartman trophy for BPP was presented to a British mare, Romana. There are also many Argentine-bred prizewinners around the world. The point is that the top horses come from America, Europe, and Australasia as well as Argentina.

80   The former was the predecessor of the 22-goal Gold Cup, which is hosted today at Ellerstina. The *Camara Diputados* is the second-highest level tournament in the world (when I played it was a 28-goal handicap limit) and is run concurrently with the Argentine Open in Palermo, which is the highest.

mounted, I helped move as many of his salable horses as possible. Occasionally I earned a commission, but this was significantly less of a priority than me getting mounted to play good polo. My recipe for improvement was always to choose the option of playing the best polo that would have me.

What are the most appealing things about playing in Argentina? It is undoubtedly **the** place to improve. And it is the unrivaled proving ground, because to play in the *"Abierto"* (Argentine Open) is to have reached the pinnacle of the sport.[81] Equally appealing is the culture of the sport. Unlike in the U.S. where polo is fortunate to even get a mention in the *Palm Beach Post's* society pages, Argentine publications such as *La Nacion* and *Clarín* feature polo on the front page of their sports section. Top players and major tournaments are covered right alongside other popular sports such as soccer, tennis and rugby. It is a place where polo is considered the real deal. Along with the press coverage and fandom comes no shortage of glamour in and around the Argentine polo scene.

Nowhere is this more evident than at *La Catedral*[82] during the playing of the Argentine Open matches in November and early December. The stadium—located directly on *Avenida Libertador*, a major thoroughfare running into the center of Buenos Aires—fits over ten thousand spectators, and is a place where the bloodlines of the human protagonists are scrutinized

---

81 The tournaments of Tortugas, Hurlingham and Palermo represent the only true "Opens." The word "Open" refers here to: 1) no maximum handicap limit for teams entering the tournament and 2) all matches played "on the flat" with no equalizing handicap administered on the scoreboard prior to the match.

82 Literally, "the Cathedral," nickname for the #1 field's stadium at the *Campo Argentino de Polo* in the Palermo suburb of Buenos Aires.

almost as intensely as those of the horses they ride. As one polo matriarch articulated to Shelley, "Here, we are more English than the English!"[83] On his first visit to view an Open match in *La Catedral*, American blogger Brian Byrnes described it as: "Quite a scene!—an eclectic international mix of jetsetters, socialites, polo junkies, gauchos, corporate executives, models and horse lovers." As a nonpoloist, Byrnes can be forgiven for failing to mention the polo players and their families.

An indelible memory from my frequent trips to this stadium is of the melée of polo players and companions *taking tea* or drinking *Quilmes* (an Argentine beer) at the long bar under the grandstands after matches. If your life was polo, this was where you wanted to be. People of all generations—dressed in anything from tweed, to gaucho duds, to the T-shirt and ball cap costume of polo pros—haggled over horses, negotiated teams and sponsors for Florida, and dissected the inner workings of their sport. No detail was too small. The mostly (but not exclusively) male polo players conversed, brokered deals . . . and gossiped. *Which mares were going to which embryo centers, which studs were breeding to whom, whose handicap would likely go up or down, the number of bad umpiring calls in the recent match, and the rumored player trades for next year's Abierto teams.* Even if it wasn't your horse or match or team—this was important stuff. If knowledge is money, then everyone left a little bit richer.

For years, I attended these matches. Initially, I was a supporter of La Espadaña.[84] I studied horses I had heard of during

Hector's campfire stories, as well as those that I had ridden—or even practiced—through working with Alfonso. It was a thrill the few times I got to play a *Cámara* game on field #2 at Palermo and then walk over in my dirty whites to watch the real thing on the #1 field, *cancha de la Victoria*. I would go sit by myself, sometimes in the low-lying *Avenida Dorrego* stands nearest the pony-lines, and select one orthodox player to study—someone I felt I could actually learn from.

During these early career years of apprenticeship and horse-trading, it never seriously occurred to me that it would be possible to participate on this stage. I was finding it challenging enough to get myself mounted on my own ponies at home in the States. But in 1998, after two strong seasons in Florida, I was invited to join a newly formed Argentine team and actually compete in the Argentine Open. Gathering quality horses presented a huge hurdle; I could not afford to bring my own ponies (the costs of air transport as well as to my Florida winter season—in terms of both injuries and having a tired string—were prohibitive). But I had had years of experience finding creative ways to get myself mounted in Argentina. And when else would I ever have any opportunity like this?

On November 7, 1999, I played my first match on field #1 of Palermo, *La Catedral.* I was the only foreigner in the tournament. And we played versus Chapaleufu I, in what would prove to be the last season the four 10-goal Heguy brothers would ever enter the field together.[85] My team (Hurlingham-Audi) lost the match 9–16, but we managed to overcome the teams' respective

---

85   Gonzalo Heguy, age 35, died in a tragic car accident later that year (on April 6, 2000) in La Pampa.

handicap difference, and I was elated. *"The feeling was incredible and I played very well,"* I found in my journal from that time.

Team Audi, Argentine Open, 1999. Ruben Sola, Adam Snow, Benjamin Araya, Matias Magrini

In 2004, I was back at it again, this time with a multi-national squad. Our sponsor was the International Polo Club (IPC)[86] and so I was able to bring my operation down there: seven of my own horses, my tack, and my grooms Bento and

---

86 I played with fellow American, Jeff Hall; South African, Stuart (Sugar) Erskine; and Argentine, Gaston Laulhle. My two sons were enrolled in a local school, Morelands. John Goodman, the original founder and owner of IPC, is the individual responsible for generously backing our team, "IPC."

Bete. The previous winter in Palm Beach we were already deep into the planning stages for this "Open season" before learning that we would need to qualify in order to join the top flight for the Hurlingham and Palermo Opens.[87] If somehow we did not qualify, it would mean that all the time and resources we had committed to this project would be for naught. The qualification round—one match in *La Catedral* and one match on Palermo's #2 field (both with my family in attendance)—were two of the most intense contests I have ever played. Because the consequences of a loss seemed so immense, putting the results out of my head proved an enormous challenge. I have an image of sitting in our team chairs in the corner by *Ave. Libertador* getting ready to go into the final chukker of our first qualifier against Colonel Suarez with a tied score. There were helpers around, volunteer coaches, friends, and former teammates all in our camp. They knew what rode on this chukker and it felt like they were all looking at me, the 10-goaler on the team, to see if any strategic tweaks were needed. And I started studying the situation pretty hard, but then I remembered Ani's teachings and realized that, especially now, was not the time to analyze. *"Vamos!"* I said to the people around me, and they seemed to understand and took up the call—no time to think now, just play, "let's do it!"

And we did it. My teammate got one, and then I got a good goal out of the next throw-in. We won that match. When the dust had settled after the two-week qualifying round, we had two tight "Ws" and had realized our goal of qualifying for the

---

87   The six highest handicapped teams had automatic entry. (At one point, it seemed like our 31-goal aggregate team handicap would be enough for direct entry but, in the end, it was not.) To make up the seventh and eighth spots for Hurlingham and Palermo, the two finalists out of a six-team tournament on fields #1 and #2 in Palermo were selected. Sort of like the playoff matches to qualify for soccer's World Cup.

Hurlingham and Palermo Opens. Our celebration, as well as our philosophy to save a couple horses for Palermo, lasted only as long as our next game. In our first match of Hurlingham, IPC faced a powerful La Aguada (with four Novillo Astrada brothers all rated 9 or 10 goals) and was decisively trounced. After that humbling lesson, we committed to treating each match like a finals and we managed to hold our own for the remainder of the season.

If Palermo represents the polo player's ultimate stage, the stakes related to performing well on this stage are higher today than ever before. The "gentleman's game" of the previous generation (up until the late 1970s)—where salaried professionalism was largely frowned upon and top Argentine players were compensated for their overseas trip through selling their horses—has evolved into a full-on professional sport and a multifaceted industry.

Initially, in the late '70s and early '80s, players began to command salaries for playing tournaments in places like the United States and England. Gradually the range of countries where a player can gain employment has multiplied. At the time of this writing, I have peers earning polo salaries in a diverse range of countries: Chile, Brazil, Costa Rica, El Salvador, Mexico, Canada, France, Spain, Italy, Nigeria, Dubai, Australia, Japan, Malaysia, Brunei, Pakistan, India, and China. And the list is growing.

As playing salaries rose, so, too, did players' willingness to spend substantial amounts of money to be competitively mounted in the world's top venues.[88] Increasingly, the best players will go to any lengths for the best horses: buying, breeding, cloning, partnerships with investors, leasing, bor-

---

88 Argentina (Sept–Dec), the U.S. (Jan–April) and England (May–July) host the most competitive tournaments with the best horses.

rowing from their sponsors—even paying air transport costs so that one favorite horse may play seasons on two or three continents in the same year. Consequently, the mare or stallion that performs well in *La Catedral*—before the savvy audience in the surrounding stands as well as viewers of ESPN's coverage—is also creating a pedigree that could make their offspring valuable commodities.[89]

A decade ago there were only two *remates* (auctions) during the course of the Argentine high-goal season (Sept–Dec), selling mostly unstarted two-year-olds. In 2015 there were fourteen. This flourishing market in polo pony sales is due to technology allowing for embryo transfer in breeding horses.[90] Essentially, this involves impregnating a mare and, after a certain period, flushing-out that embryo and implanting it into a surrogate mother who will carry the foal through gestation and then raise it as her own. This allowed for top mares—which were still competing in their prime on the grounds of Palermo—to spawn (at least genetically) several foals each year. Particularly in Argentina, where costs are low and the sport is popular, this proved a game changer for polo breeding and sales.

The Argentine polo breed (*Cria Polo Argentino*) is both a registered breed of horse as well as a marketable brand.[91] It's annual catalogue lists all known breeding for ponies participating in the Argentine Open. It recognizes these equine athletes—some

---

89   There are amazing geldings performing, too. But the only reproductive option for them would be cloning (still a relatively new and expensive procedure—in the ballpark of $100,000 for one foal).

90   Embryo transfer is not allowed in thoroughbred racing.

91   Established in 1984 by Argentine polo breeders, the association offers a permanent freeze brand of a horse's head (with ears pinned back in full-flight) that is often applied to the rump or shoulder of registered *Polo Argentino* horses.

of which have been imported[92]—as well as their breeders and trainers. After every Open match of the season, the association now recognizes the best *Polo Argentino* product of the day with a BPP horse blanket. In fact, it is not uncommon to see this award given in places like the U.S., England, and Spain in addition to the local tournament's Best Playing Pony award.[93] Similar to the Jockey Club's registry for thoroughbred racing, this registry guarantees proof of pedigree for potential buyers.

Corporate sponsorship in Argentina has also blossomed. In 1999, Audi paid a meager $20,000 to "stamp their rings" on the white jeans and gray jerseys of our Hurlingham-Audi team (granted, not a viable contender) in the Argentine Open. Today, corporate sponsors like Piaget, Cartier, Jaeger-LeCoultre, Citibank, ICBC, EFG, Mercedes-Benz, VW, and Stella Artois recognize real advertising returns on six-figure investments sponsoring teams—or the tournament itself—in Palermo.

Promotionally, it helps that the winningest—in my opinion, the best—player of all time, Adolfo Cambiaso, is out there on display. Since his 1992 debut at age eighteen, he has exhibited his talents thus far in twenty-three consecutive Argentine Opens. His ball handling skills, goal scoring, and agile horses can be appreciated even by those unfamiliar with the game. And he is an innovator. On the field, this expresses itself in his close ball possession that changed the way the game is played

---

92   Most notably the U.S., U.K., and New Zealand.

93   At the trophy presentations for the US Opens in 2014 and 2015 in Wellington, Florida, the Willis L. Hartman award was presented respectively to *Mia* (American) and *Romana* (England) for Best Playing Pony. Then, another pony prize was presented for the best playing *Polo Argentino* registered horse of the day. To be fair, in 2015 the "Best American Horse" in the Argentine Open prize was presented for the first time—to *Chocolate*, a California-bred gelding who had also won the Susan Townley prize in 2013.

(and even some of the rules)[94]; off of it, he promotes not only his own clothing brand and wine vintage, but also mainstream acceptance of the sport.[95] In 2013 he played the first cloned polo pony in the finals of the Open (an event *The Economist* covered.) And his self-fashioned 40-goal team, La Dolfina, made history in 2015 by winning their third consecutive triple crown.[96]

In November 2015 I attended *Ellerstina's Gran Venta Annual* (Big Annual Sale). Arriving jet-lagged and somewhat skeptical of this "big show" I had only heard about, it didn't take me long to get swept-up in the excitement. As the auctioneer asked us repeatedly, *"Cuanto vale? Cuanto vale?"* twenty two-year-old fillies, one two-year-old colt, one yearling filly, and eleven embryos (still inside their surrogate mothers) circled around the roped-off grass ring before us. On the large movie screen behind the ring ran videos of the mothers and grandmothers of these prospects performing in Palermo. Their famous mothers and grandmothers—*Luna, H, Chusma, Mecha, Lambada, Easy Go*—are familiar names to most polo players. And watching

---

94 A new interpretation of rule's committees in Argentina, US and England found "turning with the ball" to be dangerous—not so much because of the inherent danger but in an effort to return to a more traditional, "open" style of polo with an emphasis on back-shots and turning without the ball—kind of a "living constitution" approach to rules that were designed predominantly to prevent danger.

95 In 2002, *La Dolfina* became the first to integrate the soccer and polo cultures when they donned the black and green colors of Adolfo's favorite *futbol* team—*Nueva Chicago*—and bussed fans in to Palermo to view their matches. *La Nacion* reported hardcore soccer fans arriving with banners and fireworks and, during the finals, caused a twenty-minute delay as spectators poured out of the stands and onto the field to escape the smoke. The event was frowned upon by traditionalists but it also indicated that this was the real thing, a real sport, with all the passions—even hooliganism. *La Dolfina* won that Open title, their first of many. And banners, drums and smoke bombs are in evidence in the bleachers to this day.

96 Polo's "Triple Crown" is considered to be winning the three consecutive Argentine Opens: Tortugas, Hurlingham, and Palermo. So, winning the *"Triple Triple"* entails nine straight tournament titles over the course of three years.

them perform their legendary turns and sprints on the big screen, it was easy to conceive of their genetic offspring before us as future champions. The wine, *hors d'oeuvres*, hearty soup, and dessert were delicious. The two-year-olds were sleek-coated and full-muscled from weeks of feed and walking. And, while prices ranged anywhere from $30,000 to $155,000, the buyers could be confident in the quality for which they were paying. My only regret was that I didn't have a wealthy backer so that I could bid on my favorites and participate fully in the event.

In my study in Aiken, I recently watched a replay of ESPN's coverage of the 2014 Argentine Open. The camera panned to Gonzalo Pieres celebrating his sons' team *Ellerstina's* semifinal victory.[97] His elation was evident as he received congratulations from the mob of the team's extensive staff and supporters—coaches, sports psychologists, substitute players, trainers, managers, veterinarians, farriers, grooms, *pilotos*[98], wives, children, and a host of individuals indirectly involved with the sponsorship of their team. On this day, he celebrated the victory of his three talented sons and his son-in-law, the performances of their excellent ponies—many of whose mothers he had played on this same field—and the success of his brand.

The future of polo in all parts of the world will doubtless carry Argentina's stamp. Aspiring players will pilgrimage there for inspiration and experience; lovers of the game will go to witness the spectacle of *el mejor polo del mundo*; horse buyers will travel to find their dream strings. In *La Catedral*, the Argentine polo brand will be on display in all its glory, proving that its polo

---

97   Gonzalo is the brother of my mentor Alfonso Pieres, and is considered the best breeder of polo ponies of his generation, and among the best polo players in the history of the sport.

98   Literally, "pilots," these are players who act as personal riders (jockeys) for the top players to help with the riding and practicing responsibilities for so many horses.

legacy is being strengthened from generation to generation, both human and equine. From the estancias of the pampas to the fields in and around Buenos Aires, the traditions of polo have blended with the innovations that are essential to the sport's continued prosperity. Indeed, *Polo Argentino* creates, as well as reflects, polo's popularity; in its role as bellwether, Argentine polo bodes well for the future of the sport.

CHAPTER 14

IT'S A DANGEROUS GAME

The second most-asked question I get when a new acquaintance discovers my husband is a professional polo player (the first being, "Has he played with the Prince?") is "Isn't that really dangerous?" If Adam is present, the question is usually brushed off; it is something no poloist wants to think about, much less talk about. But over the course of a decades-long career, the danger inherent to the sport is impossible to avoid. At least once, it will stare you in the face.

Adam's first confrontation occurred in 1988, his first year playing professionally. The photos illustrate the accident: his horse was "hit behind the saddle," meaning that as a horse is running at thirty-five-plus miles per hour, its hind limbs are swiped out from under it by another horse and it falls to the side, often with a twist and a forward roll. Adam lay briefly unconscious on the field, and was lucky to escape with only a concussion, a broken collarbone, and a dislocated thumb; the horse was fortunately unhurt.

The end to Adam's first Florida season, 1988, while playing for Rolex at Palm Beach Polo.

Another common collision is "to get T-boned," which means that horses meet at full speed at right angles to each other—usually the one whose side ribs get hit absorbs the brunt of the impact. Horses meeting chest-to-chest is another very dangerous situation where horses collide head on, with their respective heads batting up against the opposing riders' faces or chests. These three constitute the worst types of collisions.

Because of the speed at which the horses travel in polo, and at all directions on the field simultaneously, with players hell-bent for gaining a millisecond's advantage, there is the creation of an environment ripe for crashes. As a player, you desperately hope for your horse to maintain her footing, but the aforementioned situations, in addition to field and weather conditions, make some falls inevitable. It should be noted that the rules of the game are meant to prevent such collisions and protect both horses and riders (as described they are all fouls[99]) but as in all things rules aren't always followed.

Adam was involved in a bad wreck—a "T-bone" with his own teammate in 1996—after which he was uninjured but the other player was down and unconscious. When the EMT arrived on the field they deemed it necessary to perform a tracheotomy. Unfortunately this was botched and many weeks later the player still lay in the hospital; it was considered that the resultant bleeding, nerve damage and infections from the faulty tracheotomy caused as much morbidity as the polo accident itself.

One of the most painful injuries Adam suffered was getting hit with a mallet head under the chin—polo mallets are made of bamboo canes and thus have a lot of 'whip' in them at the end

---

99 Most fouls in polo involve right-of-way issues—an imaginary line between the hitter and the ball constitutes a line of play that can't be crossed.

of the swing arc. It was the finals of a 20-goal tournament in California, and he tried to keep playing but the medics couldn't get the bleeding to stop, and eventually the umpires threw him off the field. After his team lost, he made his way to the emergency room. He luckily escaped having a broken jaw but lived on a steady diet of Vicodin and smoothies for many days afterwards.

The most frequent injuries to polo players include lacerations and bruises from being struck by the ball (a polo ball is made of hard plastic and travels at speeds upwards of one hundred miles an hour), or a horse head, and broken ribs and dislocated collarbones from being involved in a fall. For most of these afflictions, the treatment is relatively straightforward—a few nights' stay in the hospital, a couple of sutures, maybe a sling or a cast, and the player is back on the horse in a day, a week, or a month. Fortunately, most players now wear safety glasses, as before these were in common use many players lost their vision when struck in the eye with the ball. Concussions are a serious risk, but helmets are required and the technology keeps improving.

But fatalities do occur. During a particularly rough spell over three months Adam witnessed two friends' deaths during practices, once in Argentina and once in Florida. Both poloists were accomplished players and riders; they were just victims of bad timing and accidents. It was a soul-breaking experience, with one occurring soon after the other, from which it was difficult for Adam to regain his equilibrium. For both men, however, their families insisted that there was probably no better way to go than playing a game they loved. Later that year, hearing the strains of "Amazing Grace" echo through the Santa Barbara Mission church at the funeral of a player from the Santa Barbara Polo Club (whom we did not know, who also had an accident on the polo field), it all came crashing down on us as to how dangerous this sport really was. And after this, Adam never again asked his children to go stick and ball with him, or took them to peewee polo. These sorrowful experiences were not enough to make *him* stop, but a bridge had been crossed. He felt differently about people's fears about polo (evident in some patrons, for sure). It was his choice to continue; it was his life to risk, but he wasn't going to introduce his children to the sport or judge others' feelings about it. And, of necessity, he closed his mind to the perils in order to continue. Which is why I am writing this piece, and not him.

Sometimes watching polo, I get a little twitchy; having seen so many falls and wrecks, it is hard to keep the images out of mind. And I'm not the only one—I remember one season long ago in Florida watching a game when Adam was playing against a young teenager, who was a substitute in his first-ever high-goal match. His mother happened to be parked next to me on the side of the field, and I'll never forget witnessing her angst over the course of that ninety minutes; it was almost contagious, it was so palpable. She understood the game—her husband played—and she was too aware of the risks involved (her son, by the way, played admirably and is now a high-goal professional).

Somehow I think it is easier for the players—they are busy and in the flow, and possess a semblance of self-agency. While their perceived sense of control may be an illusion (others' actions are out of your control and can determine your fate) it is easy to convince oneself that if you're smart enough, if your horses are good enough, and if you've prepared enough, accidents won't happen. But as a spectator, it can appear quite hectic and random out there.

When confronted head-on with the danger of his profession time and again, sometimes I felt Adam couldn't truly love me, and our children, if he was willing to put himself at such great risk. But as he started playing less and helping me with the young horses on the farm more, I realized *that* wasn't really a safer trade-off. Training young horses is only a little less dangerous than playing polo! At the end of the day, I admire his determination to not act upon fear; nothing ever good comes out of that. If one is going to play polo, it is certainly best to do it without any nagging voice of caution and be disciplined in your mind to not think about all the what-ifs, for sometimes thoughts can take on a life of their own. My advice today would be: *play smart, be prepared, own safe horses, and go out and have fun.*

CHAPTER 15

ODE TO HALE BOPP

*There is a horse so good she probably single-handedly changed
my career. We named her after a comet, and she and
her offspring are significant in our lives to this day.*

"Dances with Flames" came into this world on a racehorse
farm in Michigan on May 24, 1992. One can imagine how she
must have been as a foal: tiny, black and full of fire.

She didn't make it on the racetrack—she was after all just
15 hands—so she ended up being sold and retrained for polo.
In 1997 when her trainer brought her to Florida to sell, he had
actually called Adam about another horse, as he believed she was
too small for him. However, after trying her in a practice, Adam
negotiated a deal for the little black mare. She thus came into

our life the same year that the Hale Bopp comet was lighting up the sky over South Florida. A true star was renamed and reborn.

Hale Bopp and Adam created an instant rapport. She was the youngest—at five years old—horse that he ever played in the high-pressure tournaments of Florida. He remembers about her: *think it and we were doing it, that's how she played. She turned square and inside/outside herself in both directions. And had some foot, too.* She often got called for fouls she didn't commit: referees couldn't believe a horse was capable of making plays that she accomplished safely and within the "right-of way" rules of the game. Adam would get the ball when playing her and "make a mess"—that is zigzag and speed up and slow down at will—and thus confound the opposition. She had an ease of deceleration that reminded you of air brakes on the nicest car you've ever driven.

But even with all this physical talent, her best attribute was her attitude: strong, bossy, don't-mess-with-me assertiveness. It showed on the field, where she had the heart to outrun, out-turn, and out-push her opponents. In the off-season, there were few horses you could safely turnout with her—horses establish a hierarchy when on pasture, and she would fight tooth and nail to be at the top. She mellowed over the years, but when she was younger even her handlers had to be careful around her. She was a consummate competitor.

In a thirteen-year career of playing high-goal polo, she hardly missed a game. She was instrumental to her teams winning innumerable tournaments, and won prestigious Best Playing

Pony prizes six times. Her fame grew within the sport over the years. Her rising star was inseparable from Adam's successes.

One can only imagine how she felt when she got in the trailer, stood on the pony lines in anticipation, and—finally—got tacked up and was ready to go. Did she have a love of the game? She certainly knew how to play, virtually on her own:

Calm? No, I'm not. I feel my heart pounding, but still he doesn't come. There, I see him. Now it's my turn. Heading out I feel the familiar weight in the saddle, strong legs wrapping around my girth, and finally I get to go play. Line-up, keeping my wits about me to avoid the bits and mallet heads which might come at me, and there it is—the ball. Run, for all your life. The blood rushes to my limbs, I am alive, I am meant to be doing this.

At the end of every season, after a grueling trailer trip, it was back to the same large field on the farm. Home. She was able to stretch her legs at will, and inevitably would race around the pasture with the other horses reveling in their return: hightailing it down to the farthest reaches, spinning fast as only polo ponies can do, and careening back up. Then it was heads down, in among the tall grass, and on to the serious business of eating.

Now Hale Bopp lives at our farm year-round. She has birthed and raised four beautiful foals, and has evinced as much attitude in being a protective mom as she did on the polo field. She's twenty-some years young, and looks like a million bucks: brick-shithouse bod, curvy ears, and a heart of gold.

Hale Bopp with Bento, Adam and Bete. Gold Cup 2001, Royal Palm Polo, Florida, one of her many BPP prizes.

Hale Bopp keeping opponents just out of reach.

CHAPTER 16

PLANNING TO A T

On the morning of the finals of the U.S. Open in April 2002 a heavy rainstorm passed over my house on Mallet Circle in Wellington, Florida. I wouldn't let myself consider that the match might be postponed. In fact, I turned my phone off so that I wouldn't be tempted to check the weather or call the polo office—it was too risky to let the prospect of *not playing* take root in my mind.

My preparation for this match had been exhaustive, bordering on fanatical. My sports psychologist, Ani, said "prepare to the teeth," so I took it a step further—part preparation, part superstition, always with some rationale built in (however far-fetched) that this or that would help me play better. Generally, the more focused I was on a tournament or event, the more meticulous my planning became. And this week—preparing for the biggest match of my career—my days were planned with detailed lists: where to go, what to eat, which horses to ride, when to visit the barn, whether to run or do yoga for exercise, when to take a nap, practice visualization, polish my boots, and when to phone Ani and Shelley.

I had convinced my coach and teammates to eat lunch together three days before the match at the bagel haunt that I had frequented every winter since 1988. We went over set-play assignments, agreed on a basic game plan, and decided not to practice the main horses before the finals. The note card containing two performance reminders—which I tucked in my equipment bag on game days—was considered for days in advance. Two simple things were all I was allowed to remind myself of between chukkers at the competition . . . but there were so many cues I wanted to be able to recall in the heat of the moment! On this day, I eventually wrote *"Play well"* and *"enjoy the game"* with a blue ballpoint pen on my lined index card. And then in my journal I elaborated on how I would achieve these objectives.

For the best horse list possible, I consulted with Shelley over the phone earlier that week. We were both on the same page about me doubling my two favorite horses for this match (this was the culmination of their season and they would all get weeks of vacation afterwards). So only four horses would start chukkers (the second horses listed are the spares); by the end of the match, I would have played just six horses in total. Here was the list:

```
Warm up - Spy / Rio

1) Hale Bopp / Chloe
2) Pumbaa / Teguila
3) Bag Lady
4) Jill
5) Hale Bopp / Bag Lady
6) Pumbaa
```

So my committing to the belief that I would be playing at 3:00 p.m., in spite of the thunder and downpour, was to avoid letting down. Nothing good would come from my not preparing to play, only to find that the field was dry enough to play after all. For this match the temporary "relief" of postponement was too dangerous to even consider. If indeed it got rained-out, I would eventually learn of the cancellation.

I am convinced that this same sense of "relief" is the reason why the majority of polo teams ask the polo office to start the tournament as late in the season as possible. "We're not ready yet," "another practice will help" they say: really it's fear. Competition is a love/hate endeavor for many athletes, including me. But this fear and anxiety—this caring so deeply that it can hurt—is what fires my senses into full alert on the field. It's almost like you are playing for your life. It means that much! And the physical speed and danger inherent in the sport only amplify this sensation.

Hard to imagine now as I sit here and type, but I find things written in my notes like: *nothing really matters but playing this game*. I guess that's what being fully committed means. Putting the blinders on and *just playing*. Ani shared an apologue with me once:

> One of Socrates's students asked him "how do I gain wisdom like yours?"
> Socrates asked him to walk down to the river with him. When there, Socrates asked him to put his hands in his pockets and then pushed the student's head under the water. He kept holding his head under the water until the student started choking. Then he let it go.
> The student asked him "Why?"

Socrates responded that "until the day that you will ask for wisdom as bad as you were asking for air to breathe when you were under water, then you will find out how to get it" and walked away!

When it came to polo, I was committed in this way: I shut off my phone, went back to my lentil soup and visualization, and continued to prepare as if my life depended on it.

The only debate in my mind that morning was not about horses, tactics or even the rain, but rather what T-shirt to wear to the field. I liked having a lucky T-shirt: I wore one specific shirt to the field, stick and balled in it pre-game, and only put my numbered game jersey on immediately prior to the match. After six straight undefeated games wearing a faded, threadbare red Coca-Cola T-shirt for this ritual, there was no question that I had a lucky one. The problem arose when, during the celebration after our semifinal victory, the team manager, Boone Stribling, handed out brand new white Coca-Cola T-shirts and asked that the team wear them to Sunday's finals. Sometimes I liked trying to break superstitions, but now didn't seem like the time. I considered the possibility of discussing the issue with Boone, but that would just make me feel worse for calling attention to my "crazy" superstitions.

I wasn't the only member of my team with strong feelings about a connection between apparel and performance. Before our quarterfinal match, my teammate Tommy Biddle appeared distracted in the tents and asked to borrow a phone in order to call his wife. I didn't know what was bothering him, so I tried to block it out of my mind and stay with my own pre-game ritual. But just before we were mounting up to go out for the opening bowl-in, Tommy popped-up from behind the open door of a nearby car with his jeans down around his ankles and a grin on his face: "Nothing to worry about now, boys! Yvette just brought me my lucky underwear!!" We upset Jedi that day.

In the end, I decided on wearing two T-shirts to Boca Raton for the U.S. Open finals. That I would probably sweat a little more than usual during warm-ups was a small price to pay in order to have all the bases covered!

Wearing these two T-shirts—the red threadbare one against my skin for comfort (and luck) and the new white one on the outside for team solidarity—I sat in my house and wrote down my final pre-game thoughts and objectives:

Noon, April 14

Game day. A little rain this morning and I play my best polo with unusual conditions. And the fields are sandy so the footing will be excellent.

I am ready to fulfill my objectives: to "enjoy myself" and to "play well." For the former; I will look around, smile, let the feeling come and be myself, doing what I feel and want. To play well I will breathe. This will probably be enough. If I want more it is: "quiet mind" (playing the ball with a quiet mind, try easy). And my mantra is there if I want it: "relax, enjoy and play the game."

I will use distractions to help me focus more clearly on my breath. My horses are good.

On throw-ins I will be free, looking to pounce on the ball, when I get it I will play the game. On their knock-ins I will go to EH (Eduardo Heguy). On our knock-ins, I will try to get open longish and put pressure going forward. I have everything. I have it. Just play!

After a little lie-down, I will do some imagery, mostly scoring goals. A little tap around in the backyard, get my gear ready (and bring some extra gloves and stuff in case it's still raining). I'll get my banana, iced tea, and drive to the field. I know how to play this game and I'm going to let my body take over and play with love and confidence—play with my eyes, play trusting my ball will go to its target, trust in my ability to enjoy the game (and the specific aspects of this game).

Relax, enjoy and Play the Game. Adam Snow

10:00 p.m., April 14
We won the US Open!

During the game, I recall being fully immersed, just the way I wanted to be. I have never been so acutely focused on the ball . . . to the point of crashing into my teammate, Miguel, on one play that (on video) clearly looks like my mistake. A world-renowned soccer coach once advised his side, "Don't lose sight of the ball, even for an instant!"[100] Good advice for polo, too . . . even if on one play my focus was too tight and it caused me to run into my teammate. I'll take that mistake!

I also got off Hale Bopp too early in the first chukker (she had been exhausted after ending her full, seven-and-a-half minute chukker in the semifinals with an end-to-end chase, so I was slightly worried about her), changing off of her and onto Chloe only one-and-a-half or two minutes into the game. But Chloe was plenty good, even though it was only her first high-goal season. I got a great goal on her. Collecting the ball at eighty to ninety yards out on the boards, Gillian took Eduardo, and another opponent's horse slipped, and it felt like the seas had parted. Chloe and I took the ball through the goalposts, as easy as stick and balling.

---

100   Jose Mourinho said this. He was coaching Real Madrid at the time.

Another highlight I remember from the match was mis-hitting an approach shot on Bag Lady on a breakaway to end the fifth chukker only to then get back to the ball—now with not much angle near the back line—and scoop it under her neck and through the posts. That goal tied the score, but I wasn't aware of it at the time. Then I remember a run on Pumbaa in the 6th and final chukker.

The goal-shot on Pumbaa that put us up by two in the 6th chukker of the 2002 US Open finals.

My pause on the boards had worked to create some space. We then broke fast with the ball on the nearside for one, two, three hits with Eduardo somewhere on my right. Pumbaa kept us in front, as she is wont to do, and I finished an acute nearside neck-shot.

"*Que huevos!!!*" screamed Miguel from somewhere behind me. It had put us up by a couple with not much time left and our tent–where I happened to be headed after scoring this goal—was going nuts with Boone Stribling close to the end line jumping up and down like a man possessed. Pumbaa barely missed him, but I was so connected in the game that I hardly glanced up. "You were in the zone!" Boone told me afterwards, and it felt like that. *In the game, in the zone, into myself, connected, immersed, not thinking.*

I couldn't sleep much that night, which is common for me after tough losses or big wins. And the next day, in my journal, I reflected on one more event from the finals:

9:00 a.m., April 15

*A funny thing: the squabble over who **had** to take the forty-yard penalty we earned in the 5th. Miguel ran away to fix some divots in the goal mouth (I thought he was going to change horses). Tommy moved away and wouldn't look, and was pretending he couldn't hear us, either. I said, "Miguel, you take this one." And he said, "No, you take it." I started to tee-up the ball and, with him still thirty-five yards away tamping divots, "No, I really don't want to take it," at which point he let loose with a few expletives like "vamos carajo, do it!" And then he came back only after he realized that I had committed to my penalty routine and said: "You do it with your system of 'look at the ball' and . . ." I had stopped listening and started my circle.*

My contact was not totally straight, the mallet face a little open, and Miguel said later that my swing was wristy (rather than the shoulder moving a firm wrist through the ball). I jerked my eyes up to see where it had gone—I did all the wrong things—and watched the ball sneak inches inside the right goal post! I gave Miguel an earful on the way back to the line-up, but with a smile on my face!!

My dominant thought after winning that match, my first U.S. Open title—I also won MVP and Pumbaa won Best Playing Pony—was a sense of relief that I wouldn't care so much about what happened from here on. I would and could "back-off" a little. This would surely make me easier to live with, and likely would help my play, too. I had accomplished something that felt significant in this polo world I lived in, something that could never be taken away from me. And my reward was that maybe I could lighten up a little. This *tranquilo* feeling wasn't to last for long, but at least at that moment, this accomplishment felt like the cake . . . any future prizes would be icing.

CHAPTER 17

CULTIVATING NEW GROUND

A life on the farm was certainly not my intention when Shelley and I purchased twenty-four acres of unfenced grass and trees in Aiken, South Carolina in 1992. Located on a red clay road across from Shaw's Cemetery and twenty minutes away from the nearest hardware store, the parcel was shaped like a large right triangle. Three parallel hedgerows of trees and bramble—remnants of when a dozer cleared the land pushing up lines of woody debris—intersected the open areas of coastal Bermuda grass. The long point of the triangle farthest from Langdon Road was a forested section bordered on both sides by Owen and Georgina Rinehart's newly purchased land. It was the first time Shelley and I had owned anything larger than our white Toyota pick-up truck. And we fell in love with the place, pouring our combined energies into creating our first home.

I never anticipated how ownership would alter my hitherto perfunctory attitude towards farm work. Growing up, it was understood that my brothers and I would help around the barn and on the place. Bigger than chores, we called these assignments "projects." And Dad would leave long lists of them—*fix fence, paint outdoor stalls, bush-hog front paddock*—particularly when we were on vacation from school and he had to commute to Boston for work. My brothers and I would grumble, divvy up the items on the list and try to knock-off a couple, anyway, before Dad returned in the late afternoon to assess our progress. We became especially indignant when our father required our help to complete what he called a *fun project*. "Whose idea of *fun?*" was what we wanted to know.

Often we did not have the right gear for the job. As a result, we'd have to borrow our grandfather's equipment. This could be problematic because most of it was manufactured immediately before or after WWII and it took a proper mechanic to operate. Once, I borrowed his tractor—a red Fordson with a manual bucket-release trigger to dump the front-end loader—to mow the weeds in the lower paddock—one of the items on my list. It wasn't a big deal. The bush-hog was already hooked-up. The red tractor started right up, and I headed down the hill towards the gate which, once open, would allow me in to mow the small field. The grade was fairly steep, and I gave the brakes a pump with my right foot to slow my descent . . . and there was nothing there. I stomped on the clutch to see if I could jam it into a lower gear, but with the momentum it wouldn't go back into any gear. In neutral, I was actually picking up speed. *I'm going to crash into that gate* I realized. And it was kind of exciting those last twenty yards or so, committed to my fate, and wondering about the imminent crash. The sixteen-foot piped steel gate was latched to a fence post with a short section of chain. ***KPPOWWW!!*** The tractor's bucket hit the steel, the chain popped, the gate snapped back on its hinges like a slingshot and the group of five horses—that had been milling just inside—scattered like a covey of quail. Fortunately, no real damage done!

I repaired the gate as best I could, and hopped back on the Fordson to complete the project. If I ran it in low gear and worked horizontally across the grade, it didn't much matter that I had no brakes. Even going slow, I would be able to knock off the field in less than an hour. It was on my first pass across the hillside, with the PTO (power take off) engaged and the single blade whopping away in its casement that the front end of the tractor dropped out from under me. It felt like a horse going down in front, except that the steering wheel kept me in place so I hadn't been ejected from my seat. I looked down to find one wheel clean off and one side of the tractor's nose ploughed deep into the ground. I took my time walking up to my grandparents' house, composing the words to explain the situation. I was in no rush to receive the lecture I knew was coming. In the end blame was cast on my dad for "not hitting the grease points." Recognizing this as a training opportunity, my grandfather spent the rest of the day teaching me about the importance of maintaining equipment, as we drove around town purchasing the parts required to repair his tractor.

At times, we engaged in daylong family projects. The Yankee ingenuity required for operating the equipment was part of the whole experience. Our haying operation looked like something out of a colonial reenactment: father and three sons pitching individual forkfuls of dried grass into a fence-sided, wooden wagon towed by an old Scout. The wagon was then pulled up into the barn where—using a four-foot-wide clamping steel fork—we hauled on a rope and pulley, bringing the hay up and into the loft where it could be released loose on the wooden floor. Eventually, we would fork that same hay down a shoot and feed it to the horses. Dad was never happier than when the three of us were putting our backs into this kind of work for the common cause. It was good honest work, in a region that celebrated the ideals of the puritan work ethic . . . and we hated it.

So my passion for improving our land came as a surprise. "Sweat equity," Shelley and I called our shared, hands-on work. Straight away we began clearing bramble, pulling vines out of trees, carving bridle trails through the woods, weeding kudzu, limbing-up trees near proposed fence lines, and transplanting hardwood seedlings. We were so consumed in this work that we could hardly force ourselves to stop for lunch. Eventually, one of us would run down to the nearest gas station and return with saltines, a can of mustard sardines, a couple of Cokes and two Snickers bars. This was our "farm lunch" and we paused only long enough to gobble these treats and recharge our batteries.

On foot we surveyed the property endlessly—often followed by our cat Cacha—scouting for our next project and planning the farm's development. The improvements we wrought with our own hands were gratifying. Trunks of large oaks began to emerge from the undergrowth. Paths in the back woods—to walk, or run, or ride—became distinguishable. And the small trees we had planted began to flourish with light, water and care. For us, a trip to Lowes was like a trip to the toy store! First, some handheld clippers, a rake, a post hole digger and shovels. Then, a hand-operated tree saw and, eventually, some power equipment. We purchased a *Stihl* chainsaw and for days it became an extension of my upper body—its chatter ringing incessantly—until the novelty, and my arms, finally wore out.

In Athens, Shelley and I found a small used Kubota tractor with a front-end loader. We sold our shares in the only joint mutual fund investment we had ever made and bought it for $10,000.

These early days as landowners were exhausting and exhilarating. After a full day of labor, we would collapse on our bed at the Aiken Hotel (or later, on our futon in the barn apartment we built) and take turns acknowledging that we were tired "to the bottoms of our feet." Shelley soon transferred from Tufts University Vet School in Massachusetts, to the University of Georgia Veterinary School, in Athens, Georgia. And we poured our time, energy and money into our new farm's creation.

We never named that place. Even as we constructed our six-stall barn and a five-hundred-square foot apartment off of one end, I liked the idea that this wasn't really permanent. I was dabbling, sticking one toe in to see what this commitment felt like. When a builder discovered a perfectly intact Indian arrowhead in our topsoil, I took a photo of it and encouraged him to keep it. As much as I wanted to claim it, I felt that—maybe because my college study involved the Indian's concept of usufruct rights[101]—it was the finder's property more than mine. We were not *really* settling-in, merely passing through and grazing this land with our animals for a time.

One 10 goal player had counseled me to avoid distractions "such as land investments or breeding operations." And, even though it felt right, I was concerned that this new commitment could somehow hurt my career. I knew it annoyed Shelley that I clung to my Florida driver's license and cell phone number as reassurance that I was a polo player first. My first planning sketch

---

101   The European concept of land ownership was completely foreign to Native Americans on this continent. Usufruct rights refers to Indians concept that it is the use of the land (where nuts can be gathered, game hunted, fish caught, or crops grown) which is of ultimate importance. In other words, "finders-keepers" when it came to the arrowhead.

for our barn/apartment displayed a single 12 ft. × 12 ft. convalescent stall on the ground floor with a tiny loft apartment above. It symbolized my reluctance to get in too deep, and also why very few of my sketches ever made it beyond the "planning stage."

In 1994 Dylan, our first son, was born in Athens, Georgia. My horse numbers were growing rapidly—I was fully-mounting myself—and it became apparent that we needed to expand. Serendipitously, somebody approached us about buying our farm and we decided to sell. Dedicated to staying in Aiken, we found a new parcel, only a short hack through the woods, comprising 110 acres of corn and soybean fields, mature live oaks, and stands of pecan and horse chestnut trees. Nobody lived on the place, and a couple of ramshackle farmsteads still teetered on their foundations providing shelter for mice, king snakes and opossums.

Shelley's talent as a master planner complemented our partnership nicely. Soon after closing on the property in 1997, she had created sketches, laying out the incremental stages of our new farm's development. We decided on a name, New Haven Farm, after the city where Shelley and I met in college. Under our belts we had the experience of developing our first place, the resources gained through its sale, and some strong—if sometimes divergent—objectives for the new property.

The order of construction was representative of my own priorities at the time: first, the polo field.[102] Next we built the fourteen-stall barn, with a vet room for Shelley and office for me; and surrounding pastures were fenced for turnout.

---

102   A massive undertaking that required ten flat acres of land graded at a 1.5 percent pitch for drainage. A minimum of six inches of topsoil was first stockpiled, and then spread evenly over the leveled surface; the ground was then sprigged with '419' Bermuda grass in the spring, and immediately soaked with water from an irrigation system that had originally been installed in the 1970s and was being commissioned for the first time in decades.

The polo field and barn at New Haven Farm.

Then we built the two-bedroom manager's house near the farm entrance and, only then, did we begin to consider the design and location of our own home. To ensure we had the right spot, we sampled several of our favorite sites by camping on them in a tent. One had a view, but was too near the property boundary; another was protected from the noise of Highway 302, but lay tucked down in a low spot. We eventually decided on a copse of hardwoods that jutted out into the largest open field of the property.

Even as I researched polo fields, mowers and fencing options, I still identified first as a "polo player" and wasn't really ready to settle down. I was torn: in one sense, New Haven Farm represented a challenging and rewarding venture to create an idyllic place for our horses and family; in another, it felt like an anchor of responsibility and financial commitment. I worried that every dollar I plunged into farm improvements was one dollar less to spend on a horse. But with time, I realized just how good I had it! After all, ours was essentially a polo farm where horses could be rested, recuperated and trained. It may not have been PilarChico,[103] but Owen Rinehart[104] was my neighbor. Not only were we training young horses together during the spring and fall, we also began hosting 16–20-goal tournaments which we were often hired to play in, and we shared the vision of Aiken becoming a flourishing venue for polo.

Shelley and I built a beautiful stone house among several different species of oaks. And soon after its completion our second son, Nathan, was born. For most of the next decade (1998–2008), the spheres of farm and polo were largely distinct. Shelley took primary responsibility for the former, while I followed the tournament circuit—and the sun—*playing* the latter. These were the years when my handicap was going up from 7, to 8, to 9, to 10. I played the '99 and '04 seasons in Argentina and I was unapologetically focused on my objective of reaching 10 goals and becoming the best player I could be. My grooms, Bento and Bete Da Silva, traveled with me each time I journeyed away from our home to play a season. Sometimes this was as far off as Argentina or England and, when possible, my family would join me around the constraints of the children's school calendar and Shelley's veterinary work.

During my busiest years as a professional player, I found farm work relaxing. Clipping a pasture or mowing the polo

---

103   PilarChico is a successful polo club in Pilar, Argentina, that was founded by high-goal players who wished to play high-goal polo. In its early stages, rumor had it that only players 7-goals and above were eligible for membership.

104   An American professional player from Charlottesville, VA, Owen was raised to 10 goals in 1992. He and I played together on many successful teams. And our partnership carried over to Aiken, South Carolina where both of us committed to buying adjacent farms and continue to promote polo in the area to this day.

field proved a welcome break from the pressures of tournament play. Particularly with grass, I enjoyed an immediate sense of accomplishment after passing the mower. Former 10-goaler, Tommy Wayman, told me once that he liked to ride a tractor to decompress, after a long polo season away from his ranch in Texas. And I related to his sentiments.

But pursuing this "release" didn't always mix well with childcare duties: one time, while babysitting my two-year-old son Aidan, I decided the polo field really needed mowing. Our farm manager was busy with something else. Aidan liked to ride with me on tractors (we called it our *toodle*) but Shelley prohibited any real work during those times.[105] But on this day I rationalized that the John Deere self-driven reel mower was safe enough for me to get some work done and hang out with my little guy. Indeed, this could be a *fun project* for us to do together!

The mower was a bit of a rattrap. We bought it used for a third the price, and it seems you usually get what you pay for. I hadn't driven it much. But it cranked right up and we proceeded out onto one end of the polo field. I checked the RPMs, my grip on Aidan, and flipped the lever to engage the mower blades. They engaged with the characteristic shriek of the metal reels whisking over the bed knife, but a large plume of dark smoke erupted from the engine just behind our seat. *This didn't seem right* . . . and momentarily I thought we were actually on fire. I disengaged the blades and Aidan and I leaned sideways to gulp mouthfuls of fresh air as we waited for the smoke to clear. *At least nothing seemed to be on fire back there. Could these things actually blow? Nooo. Maybe I did something wrong? Was the parking brake still on or something? All clear now.*

---

105   Our first year in Aiken a child was tragically killed falling off a tractor on an adjoining farm.

Resolving to give it one more try, I checked my gauges and firmed my clasp on Aidan's waist. I inched it forward—*maybe a running start would do the trick*—reengaged the blades, and **POOOF** the smoke billowed out of the rear of the mower in even greater quantities than before. This time I was ready. And with my one available hand and two feet I disengaged everything I could think of—stomping on the clutch to take it out of drive and flipping the lever to disengage the reels. It was at this point that, out of the corner of my eye, I caught a view of the front wheels of Shelley's Suburban as the vehicle skidded to a halt a few feet away. In an instant she was beside me, trying to wrench her son from my arms and the combustible reel mower. Only afterwards did I learn that she had been up at the top of the driveway the entire time, retrieving the mail and watching the whole scene unfold. Later that afternoon she beseeched me: "What I don't **get,** is why on earth you didn't stop the **first** time you noticed you were on fire?" For some questions, there are no answers.

Today, I do better at embracing responsibilities outside of my "polo player" identity. And the fact that my kids do not play—something that many polo friends cannot fathom—could help make this shift more seamless. Being home most months now, I have even developed some new food producing, farm hobbies. I was always into planting and tending trees, but the number of vegetable garden boxes I've built (there is some edible plant growing in Aiken all times of the year) has expanded from two, to three, to seven . . . and counting. I've studied books and pictures of edible mushrooms in North America—even sent photos to the state mycologist up at Clemson University—to identify, beyond a reasonable doubt, those which proliferate on our farm during moist periods. Thus far, I have consumed what (I'm at least pretty confident) are Horse Mushrooms, Skull-shaped Puffballs and Golden Chanterelles, without any deleterious effects. But my family—particularly my wife—lags behind me in their enthusiasm to sample nature's bounty, preferring to observe me for a spell, before tasting even a morsel.

Recently, I learned how to catch roosting chickens. This new skill I learned out of necessity, when Bento departed in September 2014 for his new job in Texas. Before leaving me in charge of his flock, Bento pantomimed this skill to me in the barn one day over maté. First, he made a sneaking expression by tucking his head down low between his shoulders as his eyes moved around scanning branches and rafters. Then, his eyebrows raised slightly as he pretended to focus on an imaginary target somewhere above head level. His open right hand glided up and forward cautiously and then, in one quick and fluid motion, he snatched across his body while clenching his fingers around the imaginary legs and issuing a pursed "schooop!" noise with his lips. Finally, his fist rolled over in a counter-clockwise direction so that the imaginary chicken within was hanging head down towards the ground. He stared at me to ensure my comprehension. "*Es facil*," he said.

No sooner had Bento departed, than a group of hens began roosting in the hay shed and pooping on expensive bales of alfalfa hay. It was up to me! I wore thick gloves and a headlamp that first night on my nocturnal mission. I got the ladder out and climbed up close, where they perched on spanning 2×6's and appeared ghostlike in their sleepy, spot-lit daze. In this trance-state, they looked quite a bit larger and somewhat prehistoric. I couldn't bring myself to go for a snatch that night, so I moved some tarpaulins over the alfalfa bales to lessen the damage from the piles of *guano*.

Several nights later I steeled myself for my first, proper "schooop." I was skittish—releasing my hold on a couple when they squawked and batted their wings—but I eventually had one dangling upside down in my gloved hand. I scaled down the ladder, dashed around the corner of the shed, with my inverted prize, and opened the door to the coop. Only then did I think that I didn't know how to properly release the bird. It was possible there could be an explosion of beak and wings when I cocked her upright, so I decided to swing her through the door—a little bit like a soft toss in horseshoes—tipping the hen upright as my hand released her legs only inches from the ground. I had imagined her landing cat-like on the dirt floor but she actually crashed down in a heap. I felt terrible. But over the course of several nocturnal outings, I got the feel of things and slowly, chicken by chicken, returned the flock to its proper roost in the coop. Mastery of another *project* with the result that more delicious, deep-orange-yolked farm eggs are available for eating.

In the years when Shelley carried all the farm responsibilities—taking care of horses, riding sets, training youngsters, being the business manager—as well as raising three kids and running her own veterinary business, it was easy for her to get overwhelmed. I, on the other hand, was paid quite handsomely to put in a few hours of work a day, and accept all the accolades of signing autographs, winning trophies, MVP awards, and BPP prizes. The juxtaposition of our daily work was certainly not "fair." For years, "honey, I'm off to work" was hard to say with a straight face when it indicated three or four horses, presented to me fully tacked, to ride in the sunshine. But she also understood the pressures of competition and respected my pursuit of excellence. In 2014 I was inducted into polo's Hall of Fame. In my induction speech, I said of Shelley, "nobody has helped me more." And this is saying a lot because throughout my career I have had a lot of help. Shelley's repertoire of skills is so broad that sometimes it was hard not to feel too reliant on her. From yoga classes, to acupuncture needles and nutritional expertise for myself and the horses, to equestrian intuition and advice about which horses to play . . . (oh yeah) to mothering our children expertly, she was the source of stability that allowed me the freedom to pursue my dreams.

Recently there has been a confluence of Shelley's and my work roles on the farm. Not that we're doing everything together all the time, but our efforts towards maintaining New Haven Farm and its inhabitants—human as well as equine—increasingly overlap and complement each other. Naturally, we steer towards our preferences—I plant trees and Shelley cuts weedy sections of the pasture with the scag mower, I paint the outdoor furniture and she bathes the dogs—but our priorities for farm and family seem more aligned now than ever before.

In 2009, we bred three of our best retired mares, Pumbaa, Bag Lady, and Haley; the responsibilities for the offspring have been shared. Shelley worked with the foals and yearlings, introduced them to groundwork, and got them started under saddle. She coached me in the round-pen for my first rides. And then, once I had a mallet in my hand, I felt comfortable showing them the game I knew how to play. Our training of young horses has been a true collaboration, and the result of this work "on the farm" is that I have three more horses to play in tournament polo.[106] And this—what we refer to as our "boutique breeding"

---

106 August 2015, one of these horses, Nureyev, won a Best Playing Pony award for a tournament at Flying-H Polo Club in Big Horn, Wyoming. This represented a proud moment for New Haven Farm—our first homebred BPP prize.

operation—represents another merging of previously distinct spheres of farm and polo.

While we do entertain the goal of making a profit on some of these homegrown talents, the prospect of selling poses a whole new set of challenges and emotions. Recently, having to put a monetary value on a homebred mare that Shelley started and I taught to play—with whom we've taken our time, and who now has a spark in her eye and dapples on her bay coat, and who turns *like a top*—is not an easy thing. But **it is** truly a joint venture on our part. We can make the decisions together about farm, family, and horses, and that part feels right and satisfying.

Bowing out of the limelight—of travel, winning major tournaments, having trailers parked around a polo field, all to show me horses—was never going to be easy. But I believe that

The family at home in Aiken, South Carolina.

adaptability is a fundamental quality in life, and I definitely have not been put out to pasture. I try to make my peace with the fact that I have enjoyed a good, long career in a sport that most people didn't even realize could be played professionally. That—even while I loved training my body and mind to be at their best performance level, reveled in the search for the next champion pony, and soared on the adrenaline of match play—there is a next step. And it's good! Hale Bopp is in a pasture outside our barn, there are my kids playing soccer around (and in) our house, and an armadillo that needs to be trapped in the lower field. The mingling of my professional, pastoral and family lives are, today, surrounding me in this place. Life on the farm has come to be my life.

CHAPTER 18

IT'S NOT A CORONATION

Adam's Museum of Polo and Hall of Fame
acceptance speech verbatim

I figured that if I could bring some of my props to this stage it would help alleviate some of my fear of speech giving. I considered a horse, but Brenda and George (the Museum curators) kiboshed the idea, so I settled on a mallet. Unfortunately, I can be indecisive . . . and so I spent a great deal of time choosing exactly which mallet to bring but I think I finally chose a good one here—and, if we have time, I'll tell you about it.

Thank you for this incredible honor. Thank you George, Brenda, Marty, the Ganzis, Barb Uskup and all of you who have made this evening and this accolade possible. Now that I am in it, I think this Hall of Fame thing is a great idea!

Playing polo is easier than public speaking because we play as a team—and I mean the "big team." Looking around, I realize what makes this evening really special to me is how many important members of my team are here tonight.

My mom is here, who always told me I looked 'great out there' in any sport I played, no matter what I did on the ice or on the field. My dad, too, who pushed me just enough and at the right time, to take advantage of the opportunity he didn't have to start polo at a young age. He coached me and my brothers in hockey and polo, and handed out lots of criticism . . . . some of which was constructive.

Friends used to joke about the on-field chatter between the Snow brothers and their dad. When I once asked what was so funny, one of them did an impersonation of Andrew running down the field with the ball and, in between shots, turning over his shoulder to respond to our father, "Dad, that's not constructive!"

The kids I started playing with are here tonight: Teddy and Bobby Mehm, Carlos Coles, and my cousin, Doo Little, who served as a model on the field and was already flying around on the field with the Fortugno brothers and Brad Scherer when we were just starting out.

My brother Andrew is here, and Phillip Lake, with whom I went on to win 22- and 26-goal tournaments in Palm Beach. And the three of us also created the famous weave polo skills drill, which none of you have probably heard of and which I am still trying to make a permanent part of the Team USPA curriculum! My 'best fan,' Aunt Judy (Little), who has made more of my Wellington games than she has missed over the years, is also here tonight.

So many great on-field teammates are here, too, both professional and amateur, and I apologize in advance for those I may forget to mention. Owen Rinehart, who was kept on his farm in Aiken due to the recent ice storm, has been a teammate, friend and partner on as well as off the field . . . and he lends me his aerator to aerate my polo field! Brook Johnson, who came all the way from England to share this evening, contributed immensely to the start of my career. He also gave me my first and only nonpolo-playing employment as a textiles broker in Hong Kong—which was extremely short-lived. Gillian Johnston is here, who, along with Miguel Novillo Astrada and Tommy Biddle, comprised the Coca-Cola team that won the 2002 US Open, a tournament I still consider the highlight of my career.

Ruben Sola, Julio Arellano, Tiger Kneece, Maureen Brennan, Cote and Martin Zegers and Mariano Gonzalez, who, I recently learned, has a new performance-enhancing technique of wearing socks to bed at night. You'll have to ask him about that one!

And then there's my wife, Shelley. Nobody has helped me more. I don't know how well you'all know Shelley, but she's really talented! She can sing, she can dance, she can start horses (literally); she is a highly-skilled veterinarian and acupuncturist, a great mother, a loving spouse . . . and is really good at helping me keep things in perspective. There was a time when winning polo games felt like life or death. But, of course, when I didn't win, I didn't die and she was the first to remind me that life was not only about polo. She helps me to keep my priorities in order and my feet on the ground.

Just the other day, for example, as we were driving in her car, I was deliberating out loud about how I was going to handle the seating for all the friends and family that were attending this event. We're not an easy family to seat, if you know what I mean, and I was all in a dither. I said, "Shell, there must be some kind of protocol for how to handle the seating at a dinner like this!?"" She turned to me with a patient, deadpan expression on her face and said, "Honey, it's not a coronation."

*This **big team** made it all possible—with a team like this, it's easy to play well. And I'd be remiss not to mention a few individuals who couldn't be here tonight: my loyal Brazilian grooms, Bento and Bête Da Silva; my first Argentine 10-goal teammate, mentor and friend, Alfonso Pieres; the Greek sports psychologist, Stiliani Chroni, who changed my thinking about sports and life; and three American horses—Hale Bopp, Pumbaa and Amy. Without these individuals, this award would never have been possible.*

Now, about this mallet . . . I used it in the 2006 Open with Las Monjitas. I missed two open goals in the final, but we still won and I played well, so I think it's a good one. The unique thing about it, though, is that before that tournament, I went to Nano's Polo Mallets to choose from the dozens I had had made. Choosing my favorites takes a lot of cane flexing and deliberation. Eventually, I decided on six or seven to take home.

So I'm practicing and getting ready for the Open, but I'm not feeling that good with these new mallets and so, a week later, I go back in to Nano's and I'm shaking other people's mallets to see if there might be a better one for me somewhere in the racks. (It's kind of like the wand store on Diagon Alley.) And then I find one I really like. It has someone else's initials on it and I joke to Irene, Nano's wife "How come you're hiding this one from me?" And she says, "Adam, that's one of the mallets you rejected last week." She called the person who had selected it and they obligingly let me reclaim it. I played every match with it in that Open and it is here tonight.

I offered it to the Museum of Polo, but they didn't seem too excited about having another old mallet around—particularly one that had missed two open goals!—so it will probably end up returning with me to Aiken. In a couple weeks, I will be packing my bags for Chile to play a 22-goal Test Match (USA vs. Chile) in Santiago. I will deliberate over which mallets to bring. And this mallet may, or may not, make the cut. Life—and polo—goes on. Thank you!

ACKNOWLEDGMENTS

We would like to thank Ani Chroni for the inspiration to write this book. We still have another one in us, Ani! Our mothers, Robin Alt and Sandy Onderdonk, helped us immeasurably by reading early copies and providing encouragement to keep working, which is in a nutshell what they have given us throughout our lives. Thank you, Robin and Sandy. We would have been adrift without our content editor, Kim Dion, who steered us towards giving our manuscript a purpose and finding the narratives to convey it. Kim, we are indebted to your intelligent approach as well as your diplomacy in working with us as a couple. We count ourselves lucky that your sabbatical timed so perfectly with our needs! We are also grateful for Communication Bloom's truly professional service. During the weeks of final editing, Rebecca was available to hold a hand, deliver a humorous punch line, or make an insightful comment, always right when needed. With her fastidious approach, we could rest assured that the final product would be quite a notch higher for having been in her hands. And last but not least, thank you to 1106 Design for converting our ideas into reality.

We would also like to acknowledge the great work, as well as cooperative attitude, of the artists and photographers who contributed to *Polo Life*. Without their representations our book would not be complete. Melinda Brewer's 2009 original painting of Hale Bopp (a prize for the mare's Silver Cup BPP award of the same year) provides the background art for our cover. Melinda also sketched the two portraits depicting the heads of *conventionally ugly/pretty* polo ponies. Kate Mieczkowska generously donated three pieces of her brushstroke equestrian art. The portrayal of Adam jumping the boards on Amy she specifically painted for this book, and it heads our chapter index. The next two appear alternately at the start of each chapter, and serve to distinguish between the two author's voices—Polo III (a player reaching for a ball) for Adam's, and Desert Horse (a windswept solitary equine) for Shelley's. David Lominska's *polographics* provided the majority of the superb horse and action photos. Ricardo Motran and *snoopyproductions* furnished the poignant aerial photograph—shot from a highrise—of Palermo's field #1 surrounded by Buenos Aires cityscape. Our Aiken neighbor, Gary Knowles, donated his time and photographic expertise towards the author bio photo and the family "on the farm" photo that we use. And Shelley Heatley kindly permitted us to use her Boca Raton cover shot of Adam hitting an important nearside neckshot on Pumbaa in the 2002 US Open finals.

ABOUT THE AUTHORS

The couple's first date in 1986 revolved around the Cup of the Americas polo match between Argentina and the United States. Shelley wanted to see the horses; Adam wanted to see the game. Since then, the intersection of horses and sport has continued to drive their respective careers and provide the glue that keeps them together. In his third decade as a professional polo player, Adam still exhibits an adrenaline junkie's connection to the highs of competition and a childlike fascination with ball sports. His engagement with the sport today is no longer confined just to playing it. He coaches

players, trains horses, and, recently, has learned to stand on the other side of the microphone in his role as a broadcast analyst for NBC Sports. Shelley and Adam now reside more months of the year on their horse farm in Aiken, South Carolina, than when they travelled the globe during the heyday of Adam's polo career. Shelley is investing more time in her local integrative veterinary practice; Adam is a regular at Shelley's yoga classes. Their vegetable garden is flourishing as are their three sons. As their careers evolve, they are still working with horses—and still grateful *to do what they love.*

32782273R00126

Made in the USA
Middletown, DE
17 June 2016